Presocratic Philosophy: A Very Short Introduction

Very Short Introductions available now:

ADVERTISING Winston Fletcher
AFRICAN HISTORY John Parker and
 Richard Rathbone
AGNOSTICISM Robin Le Poidevin
AMERICAN POLITICAL PARTIES AND
 ELECTIONS L. Sandy Maisel
THE AMERICAN PRESIDENCY
 Charles O. Jones
ANARCHISM Colin Ward
ANCIENT EGYPT Ian Shaw
ANCIENT PHILOSOPHY Julia Annas
ANCIENT WARFARE Harry Sidebottom
ANGLICANISM Mark Chapman
THE ANGLO-SAXON AGE John Blair
ANIMAL RIGHTS David DeGrazia
ANTISEMITISM Steven Beller
THE APOCRYPHAL GOSPELS
 Paul Foster
ARCHAEOLOGY Paul Bahn
ARCHITECTURE Andrew Ballantyne
ARISTOCRACY William Doyle
ARISTOTLE Jonathan Barnes
ART HISTORY Dana Arnold
ART THEORY Cynthia Freeland
ATHEISM Julian Baggini
AUGUSTINE Henry Chadwick
AUTISM Uta Frith
BARTHES Jonathan Culler
BESTSELLERS John Sutherland
THE BIBLE John Riches
BIBLICAL ARCHEOLOGY Eric H. Cline
BIOGRAPHY Hermione Lee
THE BLUES Elijah Wald
THE BOOK OF MORMON Terryl Givens
THE BRAIN Michael O'Shea
BRITISH POLITICS Anthony Wright
BUDDHA Michael Carrithers
BUDDHISM Damien Keown
BUDDHIST ETHICS Damien Keown
CAPITALISM James Fulcher
CATHOLICISM Gerald O'Collins
THE CELTS Barry Cunliffe
CHAOS Leonard Smith
CHOICE THEORY Michael Allingham
CHRISTIAN ART Beth Williamson
CHRISTIAN ETHICS D. Stephen Long
CHRISTIANITY Linda Woodhead
CITIZENSHIP Richard Bellamy
CLASSICAL MYTHOLOGY Helen Morales
CLASSICS Mary Beard and John Henderson

CLAUSEWITZ Michael Howard
THE COLD WAR Robert McMahon
COMMUNISM Leslie Holmes
CONSCIOUSNESS Susan Blackmore
CONTEMPORARY ART Julian Stallabrass
CONTINENTAL PHILOSOPHY
 Simon Critchley
COSMOLOGY Peter Coles
THE CRUSADES Christopher Tyerman
CRYPTOGRAPHY Fred Piper and
 Sean Murphy
DADA AND SURREALISM David Hopkins
DARWIN Jonathan Howard
THE DEAD SEA SCROLLS Timothy Lim
DEMOCRACY Bernard Crick
DESCARTES Tom Sorell
DESERTS Nick Middleton
DESIGN John Heskett
DINOSAURS David Norman
DIPLOMACY Joseph M. Siracusa
DOCUMENTARY FILM
 Patricia Aufderheide
DREAMING J. Allan Hobson
DRUGS Leslie Iversen
DRUIDS Barry Cunliffe
THE EARTH Martin Redfern
ECONOMICS Partha Dasgupta
EGYPTIAN MYTH Geraldine Pinch
EIGHTEENTH-CENTURY BRITAIN
 Paul Langford
THE ELEMENTS Philip Ball
EMOTION Dylan Evans
EMPIRE Stephen Howe
ENGELS Terrell Carver
ENGLISH LITERATURE Jonathan Bate
EPIDEMIOLOGY Roldolfo Saracci
ETHICS Simon Blackburn
THE EUROPEAN John Pinder and
 Simon Usherwood
EVOLUTION Brian and Deborah
 Charlesworth
EXISTENTIALISM Thomas Flynn
FASCISM Kevin Passmore
FASHION Rebecca Arnold
FEMINISM Margaret Walters
FILM MUSIC Kathryn Kalinak
THE FIRST WORLD WAR
 Michael Howard
FORENSIC PSYCHOLOGY David Canter
FORENSIC SCIENCE Jim Fraser

For more information visit our web site:
www.oup.co.uk/general/vsi/

Catherine Osborne

PRESOCRATIC PHILOSOPHY

A Very Short Introduction

OXFORD
UNIVERSITY PRESS

OXFORD
UNIVERSITY PRESS

Great Clarendon Street, Oxford OX2 6DP

Oxford University Press is a department of the University of Oxford.
It furthers the University's objective of excellence in research, scholarship,
and education by publishing worldwide in

Oxford New York

Auckland Bangkok Buenos Aires Cape Town Chennai
Dar es Salaam Delhi Hong Kong Istanbul Karachi Kolkata
Kuala Lumpur Madrid Melbourne Mexico City Mumbai Nairobi
São Paulo Shanghai Taipei Tokyo Toronto

Oxford is a registered trade mark of Oxford University Press
in the UK and in certain other countries

Published in the United States
by Oxford University Press Inc., New York

© Catherine Osborne, 2004

The moral rights of the author have been asserted

Database right Oxford University Press (maker)

First published as a Very Short Introduction 2004

British Library Cataloguing in Publication Data

Data available

Library of Congress Cataloging in Publication Data

Data available

ISBN 978-0-19-284094-3

7 9 10 8

Typeset by RefineCatch Ltd, Bungay, Suffolk
Printed in Great Britain by
Ashford Colour Press Ltd, Gosport, Hampshire

Contents

List of illustrations

The publisher and the author apologize for any errors or omissions in the above list. If contacted they will be pleased to rectify these at the earliest opportunity.

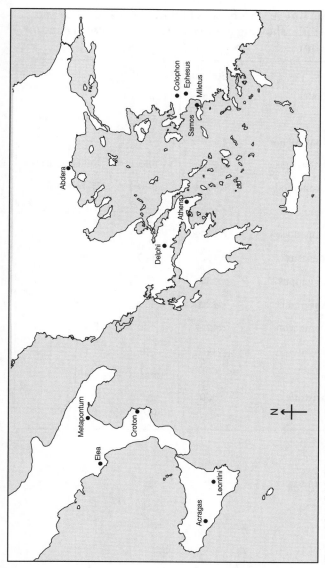

Home cities of chief Presocratic Philosophers

Time line A Presocratic Philosophers and Plato and Aristotle, showing approximate dates of writing and/or teaching

	600 BC		
Thales	c.585		
		c.550	Anaximander
Anaximenes	c.545		
Pythagoras	c.530	c.530	Xenophanes
Parmenides	c.500	c.500	Heraclitus
Zeno	c.450	c.450	Anaxagoras
Empedocles	c.445		
Melissus	c.440	c.440	Protagoras
Leucippus	c.435		
Antiphon	c.430	c.430	Gorgias
Democritus	c.420	c.420	Philolaus
Socrates	c.420		
		c.380	Plato
Aristotle	c.350		
		300 BC	

Time line B Writers of the first six centuries AD who quote from the Presocratic Philosophers

First Century AD	Heraclitus Homericus Plutarch Strasbourg papyrus
Second Century AD	Maximus of Tyre Origen Sextus Empiricus Marcus Aurelius
Third Century AD	Clement of Alexandria Diogenes Laertius Eusebius Hippolytus Porphyry Proclus
Fourth Century AD	Iamblichus
Fifth Century AD	Stobaeus Boethius
Sixth Century AD	Simplicius Philoponus

A note on the pronunciation

This book is full of men whose names end in '. . .es'. The 'e' in this last syllable is always pronounced (it is not a silent 'e') and it is always long, so that the last syllable of these names rhymes with 'please'. This may be familiar to you from the name 'Socrates'. In all our examples, Thales, Anaximenes, Empedocles, Parmenides, the ending is pronounced in this way.

It is traditional to anglicise the pronunciation of Greek names in accordance with long-established custom, by making the vowels that are long in Greek long in English: thus Thales has a long 'a' (as in 'came') and Pythagoras has a long 'y' (as in 'fly'), Zeno has a long 'e' as in 'theme' and a long 'o' as in 'tome', Heraclitus has a long 'i' as in 'pie'. Most of the other vowels are short.

There are a few exceptions to the long-vowel-rule: the first 'e' in Heraclitus should be long: some people do say "hear-a-cli-tus" but most people pronounce it short; and the first 'o' in Socrates should be long but it is standardly shortened in English.

The following chart shows where the stress is placed in English pronunciation of the main names (stress the accented vowel):

Tháles	Melíssus	Anaximánder
Empédocles	Anaxímenes	Anaxágoras
Xenóphanes	Demócritus	Pythágoras
Protágoras	Heraclítus	Górgias
Parménides	Sócrates	Zéno
Cállicles	Ántiphon	

Introduction

Before computers were invented people published their thoughts as printed marks in books. Before printing was invented their written thoughts were laboriously copied by hand into codices. Before codices were invented they made their marks on rolls of papyrus or engraved them on stone, on wax blocks, or in the sand. Before writing was invented they sang songs and entertained each other with the telling of tales, tales of how the heroes fought at Troy, how the giants fought the gods, how the earth brought forth living things, and where the dead go when they are no longer seen.

It was about that time, as memorable poetic discourse began to give way to written texts, that some bright sparks on the eastern edges of the Greek world invented philosophy. They began to sing not of gods and heroes, but of what exists, where it came from, and why. Eventually one or two of them began to write down their ideas for posterity. From the point of view of the history of philosophy, that is when records began, around the beginning of the 6th century BC.

We call them Presocratic philosophers. 'Philosophers' because they seek after wisdom, or because we can detect some resemblance to the project we think of as philosophy, or both; 'Presocratic' because they precede Socrates in one or both of two senses. First, they were older than Socrates. Many were born well before 469 BC and all but a few had passed their prime before the end of the 5th century. But second, and more importantly, they are considered to have preceded Socrates in philosophical terms. Often, when thinking about Socrates (or about Plato's depiction of Socrates), we need to remember that he is reacting to the Presocratics, but the reverse is never true.

But interest in these early thinkers is not confined to their influence on the major figures of later philosophy; they are fascinating also for their own gestures towards the great questions of all time. They did not call themselves 'philosophers', or not in our sense of that word, nor did they have a conception of 'philosophy' as a definite range of enquiries. They set out in search of wisdom, what they called 'sophia'. Looking back at their searches we can say, with hindsight, that some of their investigations were taking them in directions that would swiftly become central to philosophy – philosophy as it emerged in Classical Greece, and as it is still practised in universities today.

As we shall see, they start by asking what there is and what causes it to be as it is. They pursue the deeper puzzle – 'what is being anyway?'. They invite us to reflect on whether we can know what is real and what is not real. Suppose what is real is very different from what we *seem* to see and hear: what then? And if we can ever discover the truth about what exists, how exactly could we prove it?

When we look at the world around us, we seem to see it as made up of a lot of separate things. There are trees and stones, houses and squirrels; there are words and flavours, water and grandeur; there are kind actions and major emergencies; births, deaths, and stereotypes. All these things seem to be real and observable; all of them (and many others, too) are different kinds of things. When we divide reality up into chunks like that, we might wonder how many bits there are, and whether we could ever count them. Are there only *so many* separate things in the world, just this many and no more? Or if there are no definite natural divisions, perhaps it is really all one? Could it be all one with no divisions whatever? The consequences in that case would seem to be rather strange, as Parmenides and Zeno deftly show.

These puzzles were sketched out by the Presocratic philosophers whose work we shall be sampling in this book. The puzzles have never gone away. They grew out of a primitive interest in cosmology, but they have led directly into metaphysics, theory of knowledge, philosophy of language, logic, and many other branches of philosophy as we know it now.

It is to those embryonic bits of philosophical enquiry that we look back in this *Very Short Introduction*. At the same time, we shall benefit from the occasional glance at other, more quirky sides of the Presocratic thinkers. These 'wise men' were not narrow-minded philosophers; often they were simultaneously discovering new insights into mathematics, astronomy, physics, politics, religion, and morality, alongside their pioneering puzzles about knowledge, reality, and truth.

Orientation

This book is not a history and it does not attempt to arrange its thinkers chronologically. In Chapter 2 I shall try to persuade you that the stories people tell about Presocratic philosophy are more about what *we* would like a history of philosophy to look like than about what was actually going on. In this *Very Short Introduction* we shall not focus on historical relationships. Instead, we shall do philosophy the fun way, diving in where the evidence is rich (comparatively rich: it's never good) and treating selected themes and the most prominent characters in Presocratic philosophy in a series of topic-based chapters.

Chapter 1 introduces you to the way we work with evidence, and discusses the effect of a recent discovery of new fragments on papyrus. This brings us into contact with a fascinating but slightly neglected figure called Empedocles. Chapter 2 outlines and challenges the usual historical account of the whole of Presocratic philosophy and examines the contribution of the pivotal figure, Parmenides. In Chapter 3 we shall engage with the mind-boggling paradoxes provided by Zeno, in his attempt to undermine our confidence in common sense, while

Chapter 4 develops the theme of appearance versus reality which was prompted by Zeno (and before him, Parmenides). Xenophanes, Melissus, Anaxagoras, and Democritus all figure in this section.

Chapter 5 gives Heraclitus centre stage, with his mysterious views on being and change, and in Chapter 6 we come full circle to a group of thinkers who have more in common with Empedocles, the mystical wonder-worker whom we met in Chapter 1. These are the followers of the shaman Pythagoras. Pythagoras's name is now best known in connection with the famous theorem about the sides of a triangle, but he was also an enthusiast for reincarnation and taught an ascetic way of life.

Finally, Chapter 7 features the 5th-century Sophists. They come at the end because they signal a period of change. As philosophy became professional, its topics and methods moved on; the Sophists stepped forth into a new outlook and a new intellectual climate. They began to think thoughts that no one had dared to think before, and for this reason they belong on the outer edge of this book.

A time line and a map are provided to help you orient yourself both chronologically and geographically, as we potter about among the pockets of philosophical progress around the scattered Greek communities of the 6th and 5th centuries BC. But we shall not set out at the beginning of the time line, nor at the centre of the map. Our first philosopher belongs to the Greek colony on Sicily, and he was at work in the mid-5th century BC, towards the end of the period covered by this book. However, the story begins in our own time, with the task of discovering the evidence for ancient philosophers of this period. Their books are lost: so how exactly do we find out what they thought?

Chapter 1

Lost words, forgotten worlds

Strasbourg, 1992: Alain Martin is poring over tiny scraps of an ancient papyrus written in Greek. After months of fruitless fiddling, at last he discovers a way of fitting part of the jigsaw together so as to produce a few recognizable words of epic verse. Now is the moment he has been waiting for: who wrote these words? Alain feeds them into a computer that can search all that remains of ancient Greek literature. Will it be some poet whose work we've been longing to read but never found before? Or is it something that the computer knows already? The computer chugs. The answer comes: Empedocles, philosopher poet, from the Greek colony on Sicily, 5th century BC. The words match part of a line by Empedocles that we already knew, fragment 17.

Is this exciting? Well, yes, despite the fact that the computer already knows the line. Because the words that Alain has pieced together are only one small bit of the papyrus he's deciphering. There were lots of lines on the original sheet, which has clearly been cut from an old scroll, before it was made into a funerary ornament for a mummified corpse in Roman Egypt. Alain hopes that he may be able to reconstruct some more from the scraps in front of him. And besides, Empedocles's poetry exists only in fragments; we haven't got it all. So although this bit is from a passage we did have, perhaps there's more to be discovered?

Alain goes back to his jigsaw puzzle. What other words can he find? Where would they come, in relation to what he's just made out? The task will be slow, but it's like digging for lost treasure. For, after all, other people have been trying to make sense of Empedocles's ideas for hundreds of years, and that would always be hard when all we had before were a few lines here and there, 'fragments' as they're usually known. 'Fragments' means bits quoted by later writers for one reason or another. For all the Presocratic philosophers we rely on collecting these isolated fragments from other authors.

So, yes, the identification is exciting, because there is hope that when Alain has finished his jigsaw puzzle we shall get a better idea of what Empedocles was trying to say. Shall we not read the very words he wrote, unspoiled, as no one has read them for 1,500 years?

1. **A mummy case from Roman Egypt, 1st to 2nd century AD. Old papyrus rolls were often re-used for constructing mummy cases and papier-mâché funeral ornaments. The papyrus of Empedocles had been folded concertina-style to make a death-crown, with gold leaves attached.**

Of course, things are not so simple. For one thing, Alain's papyrus is in tiny bits. Figure 2 shows the scraps preserved between glass, from the time when they were brought to Strasbourg by an archaeologist in 1904. Figure 3 shows the best-preserved portion after Alain Martin had worked on it from 1990 to 1994. We can see traces of 39 lines of verse inscribed in two adjacent columns; this assemblage is made up of 24 separate scraps of papyrus. Besides these there are 28 other small pieces. Some can be joined up somewhere into the jigsaw. But still, most of the words are unreadable. Altogether 74 of the lines have a few words that are legible, but the legible bits are so few and far between that it would be impossible to work out what Empedocles was saying. Alain has to use other evidence. In fact, he has to use the text we *already had*, the text that the computer knew, to help him complete the papyrus lines, not the other way around.

For another thing, we can't be sure that the words in Alain's papyrus are exactly what Empedocles meant to write. It is not Empedocles's own manuscript but a copy made 600 years later, copied from other previous copies. In Figure 4 you can see some corrections written above the line, where someone has noticed different versions in other manuscripts. So here is one thing we do know: in the 1st century AD, when this copy was made, not everyone agreed about the words Empedocles originally wrote.

Thirdly, we can't easily discover how the bits in the papyrus fitted into the whole poem. We don't even know whether it all comes from the same book. These isolated scraps have survived on their own. Nothing links them to the rest of what we know, except where they happen to repeat words we knew before. One of the lines is numbered (see Figure 3), showing that the scribe had copied 300 lines. But 300 lines of what? And where does the rest of our known text fit in, the lines we knew already before the papyrus arrived? As soon as we try to work out how the poem fits together, we discover that having the real text isn't much help, not when it comes to us so badly ravaged by time.

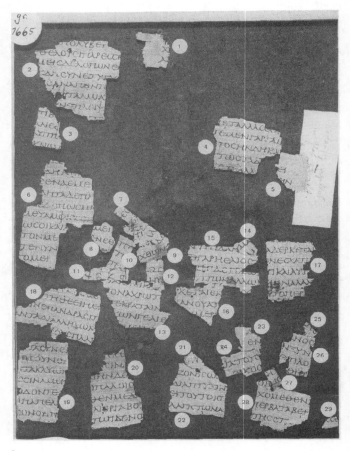

2a

2a and b. The scraps of the Empedocles papyrus prior to reconstruction.

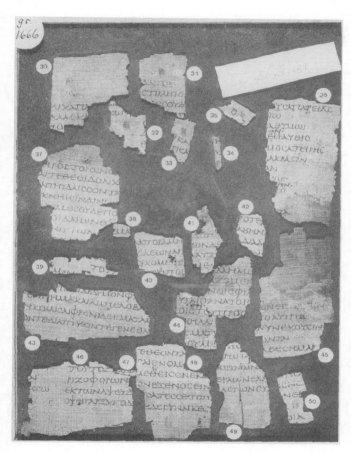

2b

3. Alain Martin's reconstruction of 'ensemble a' from the Empedocles papyrus. At the left-hand end of the last line of the right column, there is a letter gamma with horizontal lines above and below, which marks line 300 of the text.

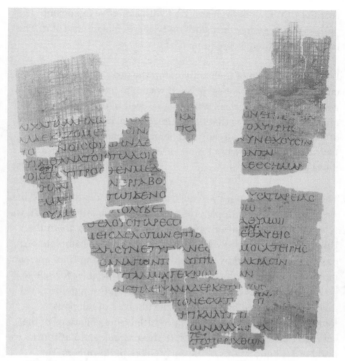

4. Alain Martin's reconstruction of 'ensemble d'. You will see that someone has noted alternative letters above the line at the left-hand end of line 5 and at the right-hand end of lines 10, 15, and 18, presumably after comparing this text with another copy.

So much for new treasures; Alain soon discovers that he needs to supplement his resources, making use of the previously known texts, as we noted above. Furthermore, a papyrologist by himself can only tell us the letters that can be deciphered. Reconstructing the work of a philosopher, so that it makes sense as philosophy, is a task for philosophers. It involves trying to work out what Empedocles might have been trying to say and why. Alain needs an expert helper, someone who can understand Empedocles's philosophical project, if he is to make any sense of his poetry. He recruits Oliver, a research assistant with expertise in ancient philosophy. Together they work on trying to make sense of it. The task will take them some time.

Let's leave the two of them at work on the task, while we try our hand at the same enterprise. If we are to understand what is going on in Empedocles's writings, we need to think about the philosophical motives that drive him, and we need to make use of the bits of text we already had before the papyrus turned up. Let's try to discover what Empedocles was talking about from those texts.

Those texts are the ones we call 'fragments' and 'testimonia'. When we're not working with papyrus pieces, which mostly we aren't, we refer back to other ancient authors who were writing about the Presocratic philosophers. These are authors whose complete text has been transmitted by the standard route, starting from ancient manuscripts, copied, by hand, by professional scribes, for sale to private individuals or for the ancient libraries, through medieval manuscripts copied by monks for the libraries of religious foundations, to printed editions produced from collations of the surviving medieval manuscripts. In these Greek and Latin texts we find both (a) quotations of the early Greek philosophers (the 'fragments', numbered according to a standard edition, by Diels and Kranz, compiled in the early 20th century), and (b) descriptions and discussions of their work (the 'testimonia'). Working with both these kinds of evidence we have a job rather like patching a worn-out garment, only that our text is *entirely* made of patchwork. Where we can find reliable quotations to sew into the patchwork, we come near to reading the text as the philosophers originally wrote it. Where we have descriptions and discussions, we can weave new matching cloth to patch the hole. Eventually, the pattern of the original cloth is fairly closely copied, we hope, and the shape of the garment becomes clear. Then we can see what the garment was for, and we can test how well it works at doing the job it was designed to do.

Who was Empedocles?

Empedocles lived in Agrigento (then called Acragas) in south-west Sicily. It was one of the most prosperous among the Greek colonies in southern Italy, and Empedocles was one of its most prominent citizens.

Scholars deduce that Empedocles must have lived from about 492 to 432 BC, although the evidence is scarce. Ancient biographies tell fantastic stories: that he met his death by falling into the crater of Mount Etna, leaving only his shoe behind to prove it, is a favourite. There are few hard facts.

5. One of two Doric temples at Agrigento, which still testify to the city's ancient prosperity. This one is known as the Temple of Hera, and was built during Empedocles's lifetime, about 450 BC. Its twin temple is traditionally ascribed by archaeologists to 'Concordia', that is 'Harmony'. Look out for a reference to 'life-bearing Hera' as a divine name for one of the elements in fragment 6 of Empedocles's poem, and references to Harmony as one of many alternative names for love, in fragments 27 and 96.

6. The volcanic activity of Mount Etna might encourage one to reflect that in the present disruptive state of the world, elemental fire must be present below the Earth's surface as well as in the heavens above. Might it also encourage one to suppose that pent-up forces of destruction will periodically break out anew, even after a period of comparative peace?

In the stories Empedocles is a wonder-worker and magician, thinker and poet, medic and mystic: a larger than life figure who drew crowds and inspired awe. He seems to have followed a similar kind of life and to have held some of the same beliefs as Pythagoras (to whom we shall return in Chapter 6, and who lived not so far away, in southern Italy).

Unlike Pythagoras, Empedocles wrote his thoughts down. He was famous in antiquity for his fine poetic style as well as his ideas about the world. Both his style and his ideas come across in the surviving patches of text, and both can be appreciated even in translation.

Cosmic cycles

Part of the best patch of writing is given in Box 1. These lines, known as fragment 17, are quoted extensively by a number of authors from antiquity, so we can be fairly sure that we are seeing the pattern of the cloth as it was originally. We can see, for instance, that the poetry repeats itself in a cyclical rhythm. Lines 1 and 2, for example, are exactly repeated further down the patch, at lines 16 to 17. And in those lines, twice over, Empedocles says explicitly that he will say the same thing twice. In this case the words recur exactly; in other instances, similar words and phrases may be partially reworked into a slightly different context, so as to say something slightly different.

This is clever, because the pattern of repeated language mirrors a pattern of repeated world cycles in Empedocles's theory. In lines 1 to 2 in Box 1, Empedocles tells of a cosmic sequence which repeats continuously: at one time everything unites to become one and at another time it all falls apart to become a plurality. This explains how there is a kind of newness about things: in some sense new items come into existence. They 'emerge' and they are also temporary, line 11. But at the same time nothing really new ever emerges. The things that emerge are just phases of an everlasting reality, and that reality is 'motionless' in the sense that it never actually goes away. It just rotates perpetually between being one and being many.

This big pattern of alternating unity and plurality is the central theme of the patch of text in Box 1. How does it work? Friendliness and strife – lines 7, 8, 19, and 20 – seem to have something to do with it. Things tend to unite in friendliness, we are told, and they tend to disintegrate in 'the hatred of strife', line 8. The items in the

1   Twice I shall tell: for then it grows to be one alone
    Instead of more; then again it disperses to be more
       instead of one.
    Twofold is the birth of mortals, and twofold their demise.
    For while the running together of all things begets and
       destroys one,
5   Yet another is first nurtured and then gone as they again
       grow apart.
    And these taking turns for ever never find remission,
    At one time coming together in friendliness, all things
       into one,
    At another again each carried apart in the hatred of strife.
    Thus in the one respect, in which one has learnt to grow
       out of more,
10 And again, the one disintegrating, more multiply out,
    In this respect they emerge and their age is not unending;
    But in the other respect, in which they never cease from
       endless interchanging,
    In this respect they always exist motionless on a circle.
    But come, listen to these tales, for learning will expand
       your faculties:
15 For as I also said before in declaring the outlines of my
       tales,
    Twice I shall tell: for then it grows to be one alone
    Instead of more; then again it disperses to be more
       instead of one –
    Fire and water and earth and the measureless height of air;
    And deadly strife apart from those, as great in every way,
20 And friendliness among them, equal in length and
    breadth.

Box 1: A key theme in Empedocles's understanding of the world,
fragment 17, 1–20. The cosmos oscillates between periods of
unity and periods of plurality, under the alternating influence of
friendliness and strife.

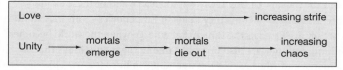

7. The alternation of love and strife is best envisaged as taking place along a single line rather than a circle. From the state of total love at the left-hand end, the world proceeds towards increasing strife on its trajectory from left to right, and then back towards total love on its trajectory from right to left. As it goes from left to right the elements and compounds emerge, as the unified sphere breaks up, then they become ever more hostile and diverse as hatred increases, spiralling towards a ghastly state of chaos and strife, as shown on the diagram. Then at some point in time the arrows must be reversed. The changes shown on the diagram are undone in reverse, as the world goes back along the same route. There is, perhaps, no fixed target at the right-hand end.

world alternately behave in contrasting ways because of their friendliness and their strife, which alternate.

However, friendliness and strife may be more than just emotions or tendencies within the elements; they are also listed as extra items that emerge as the world divides, at lines 18 to 20. Are they additional things? Do they occupy space alongside the four major components of the physical world, that is earth, air, fire, and water? They appear to have size ('equal in length and breadth'). They have a place, within or outside the set of things into which the world has disintegrated, in line 17 ('apart from those'; 'among them'). Sometimes they seem to be gods. Could all these things be said if friendliness and strife were just feelings? Perhaps so. Perhaps that's what gods were in the ancient world.

Fire, water, earth, and air

Fire, water, earth, and air are listed in line 18 of the text in Box 1. Empedocles is famous as the first person to name these four elements (or 'roots of everything', as he called them). They were to become the standard elements, identified as basic substances not themselves composed of more fundamental things, for scientists right through antiquity and the medieval world.

But the passage in Box 1 leaves it unclear whether these elements are permanent or transitory items in Empedocles's universe. In line 18 they are listed as the things that emerge when the world becomes plural; but they are also probably among the many things that 'emerge and whose age is not unending' in lines 9 to 11. This is because they cease to be there again, every time they get re-absorbed into the one, as the cycle goes round. The one is not a composite of separate things. Yet in another sense, as lines 12 to 13 tell us, the endlessly repeated returns mean that these elements never cease to be: they permanently occupy their own position on the ceaseless pendulum of time.

Empedocles also mentions a 'twofold birth of mortals' (line 3). Here he is probably referring to the development of living creatures. These, he famously suggests, are not deliberately created but emerge by a kind of evolution. They are the accidental result of the gradual processes affecting the elements as they grow together or fall apart. If we imagine the world on a trajectory from right to left of the diagram in Figure 7, the process is towards increasing unity. Empedocles tends to describe that direction first, each time he explains his theory. As things grow together there comes a stage when sufficient unity is obtained for some coherent animals and plants to be formed, with distinctive limbs and organs. The more friendly the elements become, the more coherent the bodies of the creatures that emerge; and coherent creatures are better fitted for survival. So, by survival of the fittest, creatures such as those we know today develop from earlier species much weirder in their construction. By contrast, when the direction is reversed, to go (with the arrows) from left to right in the Figure 7 diagram, the elements increasingly fall apart in strife, and the more they do so, the more the bodies of originally well-formed living creatures will disintegrate into non-viable component parts.

If this reconstruction is correct, we might get a creation, or 'birth', of mortal creatures as their bodily parts combine together in love, somewhere on the world's trajectory from right to left, and a 'death' of mortal creatures as they fall apart in strife, somewhere at the gruesome end of the trajectory from left to right. But Empedocles says, at line 3 in Box 1, that their birth is twofold, and their demise is twofold. He goes on to explain how that is so, in lines 4 to 5. For as unity increases, new creatures will not only be created, at the point when they get sufficiently coherent to join together as bodies, but later this race of creatures will also be destroyed. This is because the cohesion increases until, presumably, there comes a point when they cease to be sufficiently differentiated. When there is no longer enough variety to make an organic body composed of different limbs, that set of creatures must die out, shortly before the world becomes one solitary unit at the left-hand end of the diagram.

That makes one 'birth' and one 'death', meaning one creation and one extinction of living creatures. The other pair will then occur in the other half of the cycle, as diversity emerges from unity, going left to right on the diagram. In these circumstances too, a new set of creatures will presumably emerge. These will mirror the first set: they will emerge shortly after the world begins to diversify, and they will be initially unified and coherent due to the lasting influence of love. That is a new 'birth', or creation, of living things. But as strife increases, the new creatures will develop more diverse conglomerations of parts, until there comes a point when their parts are so incompatible that they can no longer hold together as organisms. Then a second extinction is inevitable, just before the world itself is destroyed by its own internal strife.

In those extreme moments, at the beginnings and ends of the evolution of life forms, the world will have been a magical place, full of monstrous and fanciful creatures. Other parts of Empedocles's poem seem to have described those phases (see Figure 8).

Where exactly our own time fits into the cycle was a puzzle even in

8. Ancient Greek mythology included legendary beasts composed of part human, part animal bodies. This Minotaur has the head of a bull on a body that is at least partly human. Empedocles incorporated such legendary composites at the beginnings and ends of periods of evolution in each phase of the cycle. At some stage, 'Many neckless faces sprouted', 'arms were wandering naked, bereft of shoulders and eyes roamed alone in search of foreheads' (fragment 57). At another stage, 'Many were born with faces and chests on both sides, man-faced calves, and vice versa, humanoids with heads of bulls, their bodies part male part female and equipped with dark parts' (fragment 61).

antiquity. Some of Empedocles's cries of anguish suggest that we live in a world on its way to disintegration and war: perhaps we are the transitory race of coherent organisms that emerges as love loses its grip, a momentary accident, destined soon to decay. Other passages seem more hopeful about our future destiny, as though there were some chance of a foreseeable restoration to unity and love.

Searching for explanations: how many?, and how come?

Already, in Box 1, patterns are beginning to emerge in the patchwork cloth. Empedocles is offering answers to some fundamental questions.

One of his questions is how many components there are in the world. Empedocles's answer is intricate, since his world oscillates between total unity and plurality. So at times the answer to 'how many?' would be 'one' (not that we'd be there to ask). At other times the answer depends on how you count things.

During the plural period you can count 'roots' (or elements) out of which other things are composed: these are four. If you add the motivations that govern the behaviour of those elements, love and strife, that adds two further absolutely fundamental things – though surely of a rather different kind, *we* might think; but look how Empedocles simply adds them to the list in lines 19 to 20 of fragment 17 in Box 1.

If you count the compounds into which the elements combine there are all the usual organic materials that make up the creatures of this world and their habitats. There seems to be no limit on the diversity of such things, at least potentially, and they probably become more numerous and varied as the world becomes more complex.

If you count the organisms and other complex bodies, again the numbers of such inhabitants of the world are potentially unlimited. Again we might guess that they increase in number and variety as the world progresses from unity towards plurality.

Finally, and more controversially, it seems that we can count spirits or souls (*daimones*). These may need to figure in both periods, unity and plurality. But they are not mentioned in the text in Box 1. We shall come back to them.

Besides the 'how many?' question, Empedocles seems to be answering two other ancient questions: 'How did the world come to be as it now is?' and 'How did it come to have the creatures that it now has?'. These questions had been the subject of myths and legends for the Greeks long before Empedocles was writing, but he, like many of the Presocratics, sets out to give a more systematic answer.

Again, his answers are subtle and intricate. First, he replies, it was not always thus, but came to be so from a former state. Others would have agreed here, but Empedocles adds a special twist: it will return to its former state in the future as well. And indeed it was in its present state at times long past. So there is no single, once for all, creation story; nor is the world stable once it attains its finished form. On the contrary, it goes on changing for ever. This is not its 'finished form'; there was no 'original starting point'; there was no 'original element' out of which the world first emerged, as many earlier philosophers had suggested. Furthermore, the tendencies that provoke the repeated reversals are fundamental: they are love and strife. They can never be eliminated, so there is no prospect of any end to the alternation.

The philosopher's question: and why?

Beyond the questions 'What was there?', 'What is there?', and 'How did it come to be like this?', we can detect, in the pattern of Empedocles's patchwork, glimpses of the question 'Why?'. Scientists, when asked to explain *why* something occurred, typically point to tendencies and regularities in the behaviour of things, to justify the claim that they would normally behave in this way. Why did the smoke go up? Because heat rises. This Empedocles does too, by mentioning love and strife: things tend to unite and to disintegrate by turns, he suggests. And if that is so, the world will have a history such as he describes. It's a sort of proto-scientific answer.

But can't we still ask a further 'why?'? *Why* should the world have those tendencies? *Why* might those ones be fundamental? *Why* would they alternate? Surely it is not enough, to show, with the experimental scientists, that things do manifest those trends, as a matter of fact. Philosophers demand a rationale to explain why it makes sense. They want to know that things *must* work like that, and for a good reason. That's more important for the philosopher than knowing that it does work like that, as it happens. Hence philosophers don't care for experiments designed to prove *that it happens like this*. Philosophy asks for a reason, not just a scientific fact.

Some bits of the patchwork, as we've seen, do have a scientific pattern. Sometimes Empedocles seems to be merely describing the mechanisms of the universe, pointing to the materials, listing their regular tendencies. But that is only part of the fabric. We've looked at a bit with that sort of pattern in Box 1. However, in Box 2 we've got a different patch, cut from another good bit of cloth. Here Empedocles is developing a much richer set of explanatory motifs. The pattern is quite intricate again, but it's answering a different question, a further question 'why?'. The motifs include a recurrent picture of intelligent beings, the *daimones*, or 'spirits'. *Daimon* is the word from which we get the English word 'demon', but Empedocles's *daimones* are not invariably evil. Just as we see love and strife as tendencies in the behaviour of the elements and compounds in the world, so love and strife are also motivations evident in the behaviour of the spirits.

The patchwork in Box 2 seems to recount part of a story in which these spirits are involved. The story includes alternating periods of unity and division, love and strife, a bit like the pattern of the universe in Box 1. But this time other factors figure in the story, things like freedom and responsibility, sin and punishment, good and evil. The story provides an ethical counterpart to the mechanics of the physical universe. And it seems to try to answer the philosophers' questions, 'Why does the world go through these

1   There is an oracle of necessity, an ancient decree from
      the gods,
    Eternal, sealed down with extensive oaths:
    When someone in his transgressions pollutes his own
      limbs with murder –
    One who has betrayed his oath and is forsworn –
5   Spirits who have been allotted an age-long life:
    That they are to wander from the blessed ones thrice ten
      thousand seasons
    Becoming in course of time all kinds of mortal creatures,
    Exchanging the hard paths of life;
    For aether's temper chases them into the sea
10 And the sea spits them out onto the shelves of the earth,
      and earth
    Into the beams of the scorching sun, and that throws
      them into the tornado of aether.
    One receives from the other, but all of them hate.
    Of these I too am now one, exile from god and a wanderer,
    Trusting in raging strife.

Box 2: Lines from Empedocles, fragment 115, in which he speaks
of himself (lines 13–14) as a spirit in exile from the place of the
blessed ones. The text is pieced together from quotations found
in various ancient authorities.

processes?' 'Why *must* it go through these processes?'. The answers
involve the choices made by individual spirits, together with the
inevitable consequences that ensue.

The snippets in Box 2 start with a reference to necessity: the
decree described in the next few lines is *inescapable*. It
determines the inevitable consequences that follow upon a
certain sin committed by one of the spirits. The rest of the

passage explains what the offence is and what punishment is bound to follow.

The source of the necessity is an 'oracle' (line 1) – that is, a prediction from a divine being. It is as though 'necessity' itself were personified here. It is represented as a god who issues a pronouncement about what is to be necessary. That is a way of stopping the question 'why?' from going on for ever. When we ask why certain things are necessary or inevitable in the world, eventually the explanation has to stop somewhere. Empedocles stops it by saying, so to speak, 'Necessity decreed that it should be so'. By picturing the origin of this decree as though it were a god, he gives it the power and the status to take responsibility for delivering such a definitive creative act. *Necessity* makes the world operate like this, he says.

Since the necessity governs only the *consequences* of sin, not the sin itself, there is still room for free action. The sequence of events is thus governed *both* by free choice on the part of a spirit acting independently *and* by necessity, which determines what happens afterwards.

But what does happen afterwards? And what is the sin that sets it off? The decree apparently imagines a moment when one of the spirits might betray some oath (line 4) and commit some polluting act (line 3). We can't be absolutely sure that the sin is murder, since the words in line 3 are uncertain; but presumably the oath that the spirit would betray was a promise not to commit such violence.

Suppose that the spirit has committed this sin. The decree now declares a period of banishment for the spirits. They will be driven out from the place here called 'the blessed ones' (line 6) or 'god' (line 13). The spirits' true home, a blessed place where non-violence prevails, is lost when the violent deed disrupts the peace and sees them sent into exile. It is tempting to identify that true home with the period of unity under love in the cosmic sequence illustrated in

Figure 7, and to identify the moment of sinning with the outbreak of strife.

The decree does not seem to confine its punishment to a single guilty spirit. Instead, line 6, all the spirits are to wander from element to element through the cosmos. For the next thirty thousand seasons they are to be refugees, always seeking a place to make their home but invariably expelled again. Hatred governs their progress from one element to the other (line 12). It is tempting to identify the period of exile with the period of strife's dominance in the cosmic sequence.

There are other resemblances between the patterns in this patch of cloth and the pattern in the patch we sewed in at Box 1. The four elements, fire, water, earth, and air, appear here again: the spirits are to pass from 'aether' (the upper air) to sea, to dry land, to the sunbeams, and then back to aether (lines 9–11). This describes the physical world as we know it, during the period of division under strife. But as they travel this world the *daimones* are becoming a sequence of mortal creatures (line 7), 'exchanging the hard paths of life'. Such mortal creatures were also mentioned in Box 1, line 3, not as the homes of spirits but as the regular results of the physical events under love and strife.

Here, in our new patch in Box 2, we seem to have a tale of reincarnation of spirits in successive mortal creatures. It picks up the same pattern of threads as the passage in Box 1: there is an endless flux of mortal creatures produced in a plural world under strife. Yet the feel is rather different. The pattern in Box 2 is emotionally charged. The cycle of incarnation of the spirits is hateful. It is a punishment for sin. They yearn to go home to the place of the blessed ones.

Finally Empedocles (if it is he speaking in line 13 of Box 2) tells us that he too is one of those spirits. He is an exile and a wanderer. He has turned his allegiance to strife. Whereas the earlier lines had described only what *would* happen if the sin were committed, we now know that the sin *has been* committed, that we are living with the consequences, and that some or all of us are the spirits in exile. The passage is an answer to why these things have happened and must have happened: someone committed an act that precipitated the world of strife. It also answers some further questions that belong to philosophy, namely, 'Is it a good thing that things should be like this?' and 'Should we prolong this world?'. Here the answer would appear to be 'No'.

Other pieces of our patchwork (see Box 3 for one example) help us to see how we might avoid prolonging this world. For instance, the 'dreadful deeds in respect of food' mentioned in the last line of the passage in Box 3 may refer to killing animals for meat. Those lines imply that it is already too late: the speaker had already committed these dreadful deeds (perhaps in this life, or perhaps in a former life as some other creature with 'claws': it's not clear). Yet though it may be too late for him, the message seems to include urgent instructions to refrain from this kind of violence. Could refraining perhaps assist the spirits' return to love and unity? Was the precise period of exile not fully determined? Perhaps it could be extended if the original sin was repeated and shortened if purity was restored sooner. The 'thirty thousand seasons' mentioned in Box 2 may just mean a very long time.

This motif of reincarnation across species boundaries is reliably attributed to Empedocles by a wide range of ancient sources. It is a pattern that also turns up in other thinkers: it is similar to ideas we shall meet in Pythagorean philosophy in Chapter 6, and later, in the 4th century BC, it recurs in Plato. In all these thinkers, the doctrine includes the idea that one's choice of lifestyle can affect the lot of the soul. Purity of life often shortens the time of exile or removes the soul to a place of peace. Traces of these themes also show up in bits of Empedocles's patchwork, bits that we have not yet sewn into our garment.

9. Sarpedon, killed at Troy by Patroclus, is carried away for burial by Sleep and Death. His soul, a tiny winged eidolon bearing a shield and spear like its owner, hovers just above the body. Early Greek poetry and art imagines that your soul leaves the body when you breathe your last. Empedocles's 'spirits' (*daimones*) are something like souls, but instead of departing to the Underworld, they outlive the body and enter a new incarnation on the death of the last one.

How and why

We have seen some common motifs in the patterns in Boxes 1 and 2. Can we actually sew them together? In Box 1, the mechanics of the world were governed by alternating periods of love and strife. In Box 2, the blessed *daimones* fell into strife and wandered for a period in a hostile world. Both patterns included a cycle; both stressed the inevitable alternation of periods, first unity and love, then diversity and strife. They clearly match in outline.

Yet in the past scholars have often felt that these two patches must derive from quite separate pieces of cloth. The first describes an apparently mechanical process. There the only living things are short-lived bodies, thrown together by the chance association of material elements. The second describes a world of free beings who last beyond the span of a mortal life. Their lives are governed not by chance and the laws of physics, but by fate and free will. If you look for an image of yourself in the first patch, you find a short-lived mortal creature, a body that disintegrates at death. Looking for yourself in the pattern on the second patch, you see those exiled spirits, yearning to break free from the sin of meat-eating. You see yourself straining to return to your true home and to escape from this temporary lodging place, your body.

But things have changed recently, and scholars are revising their views about whether the patches come from two separate bits. We should return to the work of Alain Martin, and his assistant Oliver Primavesi, whom we left a while back, poring over their papyrus scraps. Their hard work has at last paid off. Their jigsaw puzzle now complete, if somewhat gappy, they're in a position to tell us more about what Empedocles's poem was really like. The truth is that they've found a second intriguing bit, a passage that evidently belongs with the extract from fragment 17, the one that they first identified with the help of the computer, and with the material in Box 1. The new bit begins by providing further descriptions of the physical world and its mechanisms. That's fine: it's what we expected from the subject matter of fragment 17, and it can be fitted into the patchwork without a problem. But the next bit includes a surprise: it includes motifs that resemble the ones in Box 2.

Box 3 contains a readable scrap from the new material, as reconstructed by Alain and Oliver. You will see that some unnamed individuals are being subjected to some kind of terrible fate against their will. The motif of fate, creatures with voluntary desires: these belong to the pattern on the second patch, that we placed in Box 2. The desperate individuals heading for doom in Box 3 look as though they must be those spirits in Box 2 who were sentenced to unhappy exile for their sins. They can't be the accidental compounds that turned up in the cosmic cycle patch in Box 1, since those seemed not to have wills or intentionality.

Should we still believe those earlier scholars who thought we needed to make two separate patchwork garments? To follow them, we'd have to extract the patch in Box 3 from its context adjacent to fragment 17, and sew it in somewhere else instead. We'd have to imagine that the papyrus scraps were from more than one separate scroll, for instance. That seems a desperate move. Surely we should go with our initial hunch, and join the patterns together where they seemed to match up?

As we've seen, one way of linking them is to see the fate and free will patterns as an answer to the philosophers' question 'why?'. Empedocles cannot satisfy us by merely pointing to the behaviour of physical things and noting their regular tendencies, as a scientist would do. Though philosophy is still in its babyhood, Empedocles is beginning to feel the tug of its question 'why?'. He tries to say *why* those regularities appear in the physical world, and his explanation appeals not to scientific facts but reasons of a different kind. That is, he turns to ideas like intention, freedom of the will, notions of good and evil, and punishment for wrongdoing. The laws of physics appear to be explained by appeal to moral agency.

> . . . to fall apart from one another and then to meet their fate much against their will at the hands of a bitter necessity rotting away; but for us who now have love and good will there will be in the future the Harpies with verdicts of death. Alas that the pitiless day did not destroy me earlier before I with my claws devised dreadful deeds in respect of food.
>
> Box 3: Prospects of a gruesome death, and desperate regrets about meat-eating, appear to be connected in these lines reconstructed from the Strasbourg Papyrus, 'ensemble d'.

It's still a puzzle to work out how exactly the two patterns fit together, and what the whole garment would have looked like, and why. The task is one that you could pursue, by exploring the sample patchworks on offer in the suggested further reading at the end of the book. Some do and some don't try to make a single piece of cloth. Some do and some don't think that the cosmic cycle was supposed to repeat for ever. Some do and some don't think that there were two creations of mortal creatures in every cycle. Most of the reconstruction that I have suggested here would be disputed by other scholars in some or most of its details. Since Alain Martin and Oliver Primavesi published their work on the papyrus, every attempted reconstruction of Empedocles's doctrines has become highly controversial. It is difficult to establish whether a particular theory is fully compatible with the new evidence because the evidence always requires interpretation, in the light of what seems the most likely hypothesis regarding what Empedocles was trying to say. So the new evidence has not settled any of the disputes. It still allows different scholars to claim support for a wide variety of views. Research does not come to an end when new evidence arrives, for the new evidence opens new avenues of possibility, which scholars of ancient philosophy will continue to explore and discuss for years to come.

Nevertheless, one spectacular result has already emerged. The papyrus has restored our confidence in the *other* evidence we use for Presocratic philosophy, that is the quotations and summaries in ancient authors. Some of those ancient authorities strongly privilege the 'religious' material in Empedocles: Plutarch, for instance, and Hippolytus, both writing in the 2nd and 3rd centuries AD, portrayed Empedocles as a mystic, primarily concerned with the punishment of the guilty spirits and with prohibitions on meat-eating, sex, and violence. Should we call that his 'philosophy', as Plutarch seems to do? Some scholars were doubtful, and argued that those themes must have belonged to a *different* genre, something religious: perhaps Plutarch and Hippolytus were confused, they thought, in mixing this stuff up with the real philosophy? The philosophical poem must have been about nature, not religion.

Now we can safely reject that thought. Since the discovery of the papyrus evidence, those ancient interpreters, such as Plutarch and Hippolytus, begin to look more helpful with their suggestions about reincarnation and demons and sin. Even the boldest sceptic has to grant that Empedocles seems to have integrated the two themes, at the very least in nearby sections of the same work, perhaps even in the same section. It now seems very unlikely that the religious teachings were intended for a wholly different audience or a different kind of occasion. So, after all, we can begin to trust our ancient authorities. This justifies the rehabilitation of immense amounts of other evidence. Indeed, it makes it quite unsafe to ignore *any* of it. We can't just dismiss things that challenge our preconceptions.

So, with due thanks to those great heroes, the ancient authorities, we can now move on with a more cheerful heart to the rest of Presocratic philosophy. Many of the Presocratics' words are lost, but we may still catch a glimpse of their strange forgotten worlds, woven into a splendid patchwork of ancient quotations and interpretations.

Chapter 2
Puzzles about first principles

'Once upon a time there lived a man called Thales. He was a bit of a scientist, and greatly impressed the people of his day by applying his new ideas in real life. This enabled him to achieve some notorious instances of military success and economic advantage. But what he became most famous for was the idea that the world stays where it is because it is floating on water, and – on the same theme – the idea that all the things in the world derive from water in some way. No sooner had Thales (who lived in a place called Miletus, right by the sea) put forward this wet hypothesis than others felt the need to take up the challenge: "not water", said one, "but air"; "not air", said another, "but earth"; "not any of those", said a third, "but some other stuff that isn't really anything in particular". Everyone wanted to explain, as he thought best, how the world, as we know it now, could have originated from some single undifferentiated matter. This debate went on for some time, each contributor adding a plausible theory to explain how the world might have come to look as it now does, supposing his own idea of its origin were true.

'Some time later, however, around the turn of the 6th to 5th centuries BC, a crisis occurred. "This kind of theory is logically impossible!", said a man called Parmenides, who lived in the Greek-owned part of the south of Italy. "You can't make one stuff turn into lots of things: one is one and all alone, and ever more shall be so (or

29

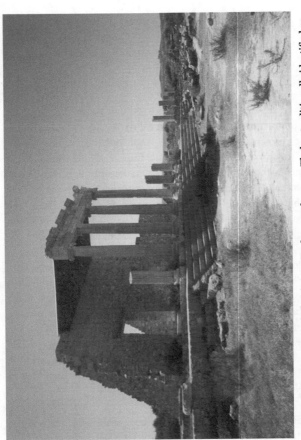

10. Miletus on the coast of what is now Turkey was home to Thales, traditionally identified as the first philosopher of the Western world. Anaximander and Anaximenes also lived there. What special features might have made it particularly fertile for philosophy?

rather, not *shall be* since there can be no future time, nor past either)!" Well, everyone was flummoxed by Parmenides's bold argument, which he had supported with an impressive set of meticulous and detailed proofs. If nothing can change, and what was there before cannot turn into something new, how can we explain the complex structures and varied things that we find around us? So everyone set about trying to solve this problem, hoping to come up with a new way of explaining the many things there are in the world – everyone, that is, except one or two devoted pupils of Parmenides, who upheld his extraordinary thesis that there is but one single undivided whole and nothing ever changes.

'So, a new stream of theories issued from the thinkers of the early 5th century, most of them on the defensive against Parmenides. "Perhaps," they ventured to say, "Parmenides is right that nothing really changes; but would it not be possible that the world was complex from the start. Let's suppose that everything that we have now was already there from the very beginning: lots of things then, lots of things now. That way, Parmenides might be right that things never really change, but wrong that there's only ever just one thing." And so they set about devising accounts of how the world might have originated in the form of lots of kinds of matter: one said that there were four elements, another that there were infinitely many, another that there were atomic particles of matter too small for us to see; but what they all suggested in unison was that even if the microscopic bits and pieces don't ever change, still by moving them around you can get mixtures and structures in lots of different forms. In this way we can explain how the structures observable in the world are always changing in ways that still seem reasonable even if you believe Parmenides.

'So after two centuries of debate on the nature of the world, they laid their difficulties to rest and the period of early Greek cosmology drew to a close. The time was ripe for a new kind of question, this time about human life and moral values. Enter Socrates and the Sophists.'

This story is, roughly speaking, the story that has been told in modern textbooks in English about early Greek philosophy for a very long time. It is an attractive and plausible story for lots of reasons. First, it is systematic and neat: it divides the period before Socrates into three phases, with Parmenides in the middle, and it characterizes each phase with a particular approach to a common problem. The philosophers did not pursue a jumble of different projects but were engaged in a single search for an answer to a single question. Looking back at the past we like to be able to rationalize and explain.

A second reason for favouring this story is that it tells of progress over time. As historians of philosophy we like to explain why one thing happened after another, and we need to point to events that precipitate change. We want to see how later events can be explained by earlier ones. The story told above does this very nicely: it explains why the thinkers after Parmenides took a different line from those before Parmenides, and it suggests that in learning to cope with the difficulties raised by Parmenides they had discovered some important truths and improved their methods of inquiry. So the story appeals to us as history, particularly if we expect history to be marked by progress.

A third reason for liking the story is that it appears to be about philosophy. Two things we think peculiarly vital to philosophy are: first, a willingness to debate in an open way with those who disagree, acknowledging that there are other views that must be addressed; and second, the need to argue your case in terms that the opponent understands, and to respect good arguments on the other side. On this traditional story about Presocratic philosophy we can persuade ourselves that both these things were happening. The thinkers may be primitive, and their questions may be rather quaint, but they were (apparently) disagreeing with each other – challenging and responding, one after the other, in a slow-motion debate. Furthermore, although they didn't all make great use of reasoned argument, they do seem to have noticed the proofs that

11. In his famous fresco, *The School of Athens*, Raphael portrays philosophers of different generations timelessly engaged in debate of the kind that is characteristic of Western philosophy as we now conceive it. In this detail the Arab philosopher Averroës (AD 1126–98) peers over the shoulder of Pythagoras (*c.*570–530 BC), who studiously ignores the efforts of Parmenides (*c.*500 BC) to draw attention to what he has written in his book. Heraclitus (*c.*500 BC) leans nonchalantly on a stone writing desk, scribbling his esoteric sayings, while Francesco Maria della Rovere (1490–1538), duke of Urbino in central Italy, eavesdrops from behind the group. A pupil of Pythagoras holds out a blackboard showing Pythagorean harmonics and the tetraktys (for which see Chapter 6).

Parmenides had provided for his views. They seem to have felt the need to respect those proofs and to grant the truth of the conclusions of a valid argument. So if Parmenides proved that change was not possible, his opponents could not just carry on assuming that it was. The fact that they seem to have eliminated it from their theories suggests that they recognized reasoned argument, even if, as was often the case, they were still doing little to defend their own views.

Historians of philosophy have always looked back at the past to reassure themselves that earlier thinkers were on the way to discovering the things we now believe. The story above was told by 20th-century philosophers in the belief that the Presocratics too were striving to be philosophers like them and to engage rationally in a dialectical exchange of views. That is, probably, the only charitable way to approach the task of reconstructing the past. In this book, too, we shall try to bring order to our understanding of the first philosophers by devising a story. As always, we shall have to do this in the light of what we take to be philosophically interesting in their work.

Let's just think a bit more about the story told above (which I'll call 'the first principles story'). In Box 4 is a list of the major figures who appear in the first principles story, and the proposed first principles for which they are recorded in that story. It starts with Thales and his ideas about water; it ends with Democritus and his ideas about atoms. Half way down comes the giant figure of Parmenides, splitting the story neatly into two halves.

According to this story, people after Parmenides gave up naming one original element; they had a choice, instead, either to adopt Parmenides's uncompromising position of unchanging unity (as did Zeno and Melissus), or to prefer a permanent plurality (as Empedocles, Anaxagoras, and the atomists did).

Still we must ask whether things are quite so clear as this. In

Thinker	First principles
Thales	Water
Anaximander	Indefinite stuff
Anaximenes	Air
Heraclitus	Fire
Parmenides	THE ONE
Zeno	The one
Melissus	The one
Empedocles	Earth, air, fire, and water
Anaxagoras	Numerous infinitely divisible components
Leucippus and Democritus	Numerous indivisible components (atoms), and the void

Box 4: Presocratic philosophers who fit into the first principles story: each one tried to explain the world, its origins and its behaviour, with reference to the first principles listed in the right column.

Chapter 1 we saw that Empedocles's main theme was to proclaim that the world was both many and one, sometimes one and sometimes many in an endless cycle of change. But this is not how he figures in the table in Box 4. Empedocles came after Parmenides and the first principles story insists, to make sense of the history, that thinkers after Parmenides were *either* 'monists', committed to the permanent existence of just one unchanging entity, *or* pluralists, committed to the permanent existence of several distinct things. But as we saw in Chapter 1, Empedocles insisted, in terms that cannot be disputed, that these alternatives take turns successively. He opted for *both* monism *and* pluralism.

Can the first principles story afford to notice this? Clearly not, for it would undermine the pattern. It tells us instead that Empedocles was a pluralist, and that he accepted that Parmenides had proved that there could be no real change. To fit the story, his proclamation of 'the one' is quite forgotten, and he is presented as opting for permanent plurality, four unchanging elements. So the first principles story accounts for only part of the evidence.

Box 4 must also be selective about the thinkers and the range of theories that it includes within its narrative. Box 5 shows a list of the main thinkers whom we might have wanted to include, and the views for which we would need to account, if we were to give a systematic survey of all the intellectual activity in the Greek world during this time.

The left-hand column of Box 5 shows what was in the first principles story. It included some of the giants among the early Greek philosophers, but not by any means all of them. It mentioned some of the things that they said, but not very many, even of the bits that we know. So the effect of telling that story was to privilege certain thinkers, and to privilege their views on a limited range of topics – as though those were their most important ideas. It marginalized one of the most famous thinkers, Pythagoras, because unless you could count his interest in numbers as a kind of cosmology, he did not fit into the first principles story at all. And, along with Pythagoras, it sidelined Xenophanes, Empedocles, and even Heraclitus because so little of what they said seemed to be about physics. But all of these marginalized characters had been innovators, and immensely influential before the 20th century.

What about the idea that these thinkers fell into a neat chronological sequence? Can we believe that? Well, it looks neat in

Included in the story	Not included	Suppressed
Thales's views on material stuff	Thales's views on subterranean support	
Anaximander's views on material stuff	Anaximander's views on earth's stability	
Anaximenes's views on material stuff	Anaximenes's views on subterranean support	
	Xenophanes's views on religion and on knowledge	
	Pythagoras and Pythagoreans	
Heraclitus (a few fragments on fire)	Heraclitus's work on morality	Heraclitus's work on unity and plurality
Parmenides (the Way of Truth)		The second part of Parmenides's poem
Empedocles's four element theory	Empedocles's work on religion and morality	Empedocles's one/many oscillation
Anaxagoras's mixture theory		
Democritus's atomic theory	Democritus's work on morality and knowledge	
	The Sophists	

Box 5

37

> *Heraclitus (fragment 103):* Common are the start and the end on the outline of a circle.
>
> *Parmenides (fragment 5):* Common for me is the point from which I start; for to that point I shall return again.
>
> *Heraclitus (fragment 51):* They do not understand how it conforms with itself by differing from itself, a backward-turning stringing like that of a bow or a lyre.
>
> *Parmenides (fragment 6, 6–9):* They are borne about, blind, deaf, mind-boggled, undiscriminating tribes, for whom being and non-being are thought of as the same and not the same; all their paths are backward-turning.
>
> **Box 6: Echoes of Parmenides in Heraclitus, or echoes of Heraclitus in Parmenides?**

the story (and in the time line at the front of this book) because the story is what determines the dates. In fact, we don't know precisely when most of these philosophers were at work, either absolutely or relative to each other, and we have no idea whether they read each other's work. They may have made their work public in dribs and drabs, sometimes as written texts, sometimes orally as lectures or recitations. So we should not expect a simple sequence, with one thinker publishing all his work after another had finished. It seems that Heraclitus and Parmenides echoed each other's words (Box 6), but it is hard to tell whether they were the words of Heraclitus echoed by Parmenides, or the words of Parmenides echoed by Heraclitus.

Of course, the first principles story tells us that it would have been Parmenides reacting to Heraclitus because in that story Heraclitus was unaware of Parmenides's devastating objections to plurality and change. But suppose Heraclitus came after Parmenides: what then? Why, then we have to tell a quite different story, one in which Heraclitus probably seems as major a figure as Parmenides. Perhaps his suggestions were intended to offer alternatives that avoided Parmenides's objections?

In the remaining chapters in this book we shall try to discover what *other* stories we might want to tell, so as to give their due to the ones who never fitted very comfortably into the first principles story.

Who was Parmenides?

Whether or not we believe it, the first principles story finds its hero in Parmenides. So what exactly did Parmenides do, and why was it so important?

The battle-hardened proof

One thing that gains Parmenides a philosophers' merit-award, as the first principles story explained, is the idea of proving his point. Like others at the time, he wrote in magnificent poetry. That was nothing new and nothing strange. But what he wrote didn't just sound good or seem plausible; it also took the reader step by step through an argument. It aimed to demonstrate, without a shadow of doubt, that the conclusion had to be true if the initial assumptions were correct. In order to do this Parmenides had to invent a new vocabulary for logical thought, because no one had ever talked about proving things before. The new vocabulary was poetic and creative in many ways, and it sounds quaintly archaic to ears attuned to modern logic, but we have to remember that it is the work of a pioneer. Part of his most famous passage of argument, known as fragment 8, appears in Box 7.

The last line of the passage draws a conclusion from what has gone before: Parmenides tells us that development (that is, a beginning or origin of something new) has been extinguished and the opposite, ceasing to exist or being destroyed, is something we can't hear. Parmenides describes what he has achieved in the previous passage of argument as if it changed the way the world is, as though

1   Only one story of a path
    remains, that it is. On this there are signs –
    a great many – that being without origin it is also
        indestructible,
    whole, of one kind, unwavering and complete.
5   Nor used it to be, nor will it be, since now it is together
        entire,
    one, continuous; for what birth will you discover for it?
    Increased how and from where? Not from non-being
        shall I permit you
    to say, nor to think; for it is not sayable nor thinkable
    that it is not. But what need would have impelled it
10 later rather than earlier, to develop, beginning from
        nothing?
    Thus is it essential that it either absolutely be or not.
    Nor will the force of belief allow for anything else
    To arise from what is, besides itself. For this reason
        justice
    does not relax the fetters to free it either to begin or to
        cease
15 but keeps it; and the crux about these lies in this:
    is it or isn't it? But the verdict has been given, as it had
        to be,
    to let go the latter option unthought and unnamed
    (for it is not a true path), but judge the other to be and to
        be genuine.
    And how could what is be later destroyed? And how
        would it arise?
20 For if it once arises, it is not, nor if sometime it is going
        to be.
    So development is extinguished and destruction silenced.

Box 7: Parmenides, fragment 8.1–21, the first known attempt at
systematic proof in Western philosophy.

it eliminated or extinguished processes of creation and destruction. What he has in fact done is attempt to show that such things *cannot occur*, are impossible. To express these ideas Parmenides has to invent a range of terms to signify what can and can't happen: he speaks of *justice* (line 13) as though the rules were rules of morality or propriety; he speaks of *need* impelling things to happen, and force *denying something permission* (lines 9 and 12). The *fetters* in which justice holds things (line 14) are another image for impossibility, and various things are said to be *unspeakable, ruled out,* or *disallowed*. By using these words, Parmenides seems to be trying to convey the strength and force of his argument, which prevents us from believing or thinking certain things: the language is being stretched to invent, for the first time, the notion of logical force, where an argument is strong and binds us to accept its conclusion. We also need the notion of logical impossibility, and the idea that the necessity of one conclusion leads to the impossibility of the alternative. Of course, Parmenides, making up words to express these ideas for the first time, has to use concepts that belong to other areas of life in which other kinds of necessity or rules apply. But it is worth thinking about how we convey these ideas in English. Do we still use images borrowed from other bits of life? We still talk about how *strong* an argument is, how it *compels* us to believe, and how we are *obliged to*, or *need to*, or *must*, *accept* a necessary entailment. Nothing has changed since Parmenides first borrowed these terms for expressing the cogency of logical reasoning, except that they have become very familiar.

Nothing ever changes

As we have seen, Parmenides concludes that, logically, what there now is can't ever have begun to be nor can it ever cease to be. Does his argument really work? Let's take a look at it. Following a brief summary of the points he intends to make, Parmenides's real argument starts at line 6 of the passage. Here he asks about the origin of something: where could it arise from? The first option to consider is that what we now encounter perhaps arose from 'non-being': did what is come from 'what is not'? 'No,' says Parmenides, 'you should not think that, because you are not allowed to think or say "it is not".' A further consideration adds to the weight against this: 'what could have made it happen?' he asks, if it came from non-being?

The second option, canvassed at line 12, is that it arose from something that already had being, so that something besides what is there already arises from what is there before. This also, Parmenides suggests, is not to be allowed. And thirdly, he tells us that we are not to accept that what now is can cease to be, for reasons that are summed up in line 20: if something has a beginning or an end then at some point we have to say of it, not that it is, but that it is not, or is not right now (though it will be or was).

Much of this is rather puzzling. For a start, we cannot really be sure *what* Parmenides is talking about. Whatever it is, we seem to be permitted – logically, presumably – only ever to say 'is' about it, and never 'is not'. Parmenides offers us a stark choice at line 15: 'the crux is this: Is it, or isn't it?' and he answers decisively that the choice has already been made, to allow the only thinkable route to be that it is, and not that it isn't. And it then follows, since logic prevents us from admitting that it is not, that there can be no point in the past or the future at which 'is not' is true.

Parmenides will go on to produce further arguments, in the rest of fragment 8, founded on this basis. These aim to show that there can be no variation in quality among things, and no variation over time, since these involve attributing differences to things, and that amounts to saying of something that it *is not*, in some respect, what something else, at another time or in another place, *is*. But what is, for Parmenides, just *is*, and we cannot say it *is* this and *is not* that, or is more here and less there.

As far as we can see, Parmenides's argument is quite general: it is not just applied to this or that, in such a way that we find that *each thing* is permanent and undivided. More radically still, because nothing can have qualities that another thing lacks (since that would be to say that this *is not* like that), *everything* must be uniform and permanent for ever (though there is no forever, since time cannot change). There is, it seems, just *one* whole undifferentiated unity, and it does nothing except exist. It is as if we don't need to know, after all, *what* Parmenides was talking about to begin with. In English, we needed a noun to serve as the subject for the verb 'is', so we translated Parmenides's one-word phrase 'is' by a two-word phrase 'it is', and then we found ourselves wondering what *it* is. But by the end of the argument, we realize, it might as well be anything, since the only thing we can ever properly say about it is that it is.

We might also wonder what exactly Parmenides intended by 'is'. When he says that we have to choose absolutely between saying 'is' and saying 'is not', does he mean to rule out all the ordinary ways that we use 'is not', like 'smoking is not permitted', 'wine is not expensive', or 'life is not a holiday'? Or does he use the word 'is' just to mean 'exists', so that what we must not say is 'dragons don't exist'? It might be tempting to think he means 'exists' because he keeps using the word 'is' by itself: he says we cannot think 'it is not', not that we cannot think 'it is not blue', and it might seem puzzling why we mustn't think 'it is not blue'. But actually it is equally puzzling why we should not think 'Tom Sawyer does not exist', or 'Tom Sawyer is not real', so the argument looks no more convincing if we read 'is' as 'exists' than it is if we take it to mean that all statements that include the word 'is' must be positive assertions not negative ones. Yet Parmenides himself seems to use negative statements. There are several in the text in Box 7. Perhaps he has to use those ways of talking even though they are being used to outlaw the very language they are expressed in, like a ladder that you climb up before kicking it away?

Should we be impressed by Parmenides's logic? If we look back to Box 7 we can see hints of several arguments against creation that seem quite good. For instance, it is surely right to ask what reason would have brought a thing to begin at one point rather than another, if there was nothing there before to make it happen. That seems to be the point in lines 9 to 10. And where could it come from, if there is nothing else (including no other place, or indeed no place at all)? Parmenides asks that question at line 7. Again, perhaps there is something in the point at line 12, which suggests that it would be odd to suppose that a thing comes into being from something that already has being: so what is new, if the thing before had being already? Is there something else then, besides what has being, something else that has now come into being? But surely there is nothing else besides what has being.

Perhaps it is this last thought that leads Parmenides to his real crux: you have to decide, he says at line 15. Either something does have being or it doesn't. If it does, it can't come into being because it is already. If it doesn't, it can't come into being because why should it? And if something else comes on the scene besides what is there already, then, if it has being, it is exactly the same, in respect of its being, as what was there already. And if it doesn't have being, it is nothing and you can forget it. Ultimately it is this 'all or nothing' idea of what it is to be, or to be real, that gets Parmenides's astonishing argument going, and leads him to conclude that nothing varies in any way across space or time. What is just *is*, and it can't be anything else.

Talking about change

Of course, people tend to want to qualify the kind of being that things in the world have got, and to say this one is large, this one small, this one is blue and that one is green, this one is wooden and this one is bronze. But no, Parmenides insists, those are not real differences. There is no difference in the extent to which something has being: its colour has nothing to do with it, and if variations in size mean variations in quantity of being they are just a muddle. Either a thing is or it isn't: it can't have more or less being than something else, Parmenides protests.

> 36   For nothing else either is or will be
>
>   besides what is, since fate has fettered it
>
>   to be whole and motionless. To this all names are to be
>   referred,
>
>   the names that mortals have laid down believing them to
>   be authentic,
>
> 40   'coming to be' and 'passing away', 'being' and 'not being',
>
>   and 'changing place' and 'switching through bright
>   colour'.
>
> **Box 8: Parmenides, fragment 8, lines 36 to 41.**

In the lines in Box 8 we see Parmenides suggesting that the language that we mortals use – implying that things change or move or alter in one way or another – is just a convention. Or rather the goddess suggests this, for Parmenides narrates his whole poem as the story of a young man's visit to a female divinity who enlightens him about the nature of reality. Reality is much simpler than people think, Parmenides's goddess maintains: just the one whole motionless thing that is 'what is' or 'being'.

And the world we live in: what about that?

So far Parmenides has urged us to abandon all our ordinary views of the world, and to go for a radical slimming down of our ontology: very little of what we thought was real can be real. Most of our entities are ruled out of existence by the stringent logic of Parmenides's 'Way of Truth'.

But besides the Way of Truth, which has been our focus so far, Parmenides told of another path which, in the poem, his goddess ascribed to 'mortal beliefs', and which we have come to know as the 'Way of Seeming'. There we find an account of how things *seem to be,* even though they can't actually be true, as we've just seen. In so far as we can reconstruct the rather poorly preserved evidence for this part of the poem, Parmenides appears to have provided a complete cosmological theory, explaining the physical world and its processes, and based on the assumption of two opposed principles known as 'fire' and 'night'. The scientific and causal theories that he offered in this section seem to be thorough and advanced. They included theses about psychology, embryology, and astronomy. One fragment reveals that Parmenides had discovered that the moon reflects the light of the sun.

Could Parmenides be committed to producing good science? In his Way of Truth, he seemed to say that logic rules out such enquiries. But then in the Way of Seeming he put forward a fine set of theories of his own, worthy of respect and ahead of their time in many ways. So what are we, the readers, meant to think? Is the Way of Seeming a total waste of time? Or is there some credit to be gained from entering the competition for 'best account of the physical world', even if you know the physical world is a misrepresentation of reality?

Generations of scholars have pored over the texts to try to answer this inscrutable question. Some of the key texts at issue appear in Box 9.

We might try to appeal to these texts to resolve the following questions:

(a) What exactly does Parmenides's goddess mean when she tells the youth in the poem that he needs to hear about the mortal beliefs as well?
(b) Which are the two routes she warns him to avoid?
(c) Is the second false route wrong for a different reason from the first one?
(d) What is the mistake made by the mortals when they posit two forms?, and
(e) what competitive situation is the youth engaged in, whereby it is important that he be able to keep ahead of others in the cosmology game?

Fragment 1. 28–32

But I want you to learn all things –
both the unshaken heart of well-rounded truth
and the beliefs of mortals, in which there is no true trust.
But still you will learn these things too: how what they
   believe
needs truly to be, persisting throughout and through all.

Fragment 2

But come, I shall tell you – take my word to heart when you
   hear it –
which are the sole routes of enquiry to think of:
one that it is and that there is no not being
is the path of persuasion, for it tracks truth,
the other that it is not and the necessity is that it not be,
which I say is a route quite beyond comprehension . . .

Fragment 6. 3–5

For first from that route of enquiry I restrain you,
and then secondly from that one which mortals who know
   nothing
wander, two headed . . .

Fragment 7. 2–6

Restrain your thought from this route of enquiry,
and do not let accustomed habit drag you down that route
to scatter your unseeing eye, your echoing ear and tongue;
but judge by reason the battle-hardened proof
proclaimed by me . . .

Fragment 8. 50–54, 60–61

With that I cease from the believable argument and thought
about truth; from here on learn the beliefs of mortals,
listening to the deceptive world of my poetry.

There seems no doubt that Parmenides saw the Way of Truth as
logically superior to the Way of Seeming. He implied that the Way
of Seeming was unsustainable on any rigorous metaphysical
analysis. But could it still have some instrumental value, as a way of
understanding the phenomena? And might it explain them more
effectively than rival accounts in the same field? The goddess
appeared to deny that it could be true (fragment 1 and 8.50–54 in
Box 9). But perhaps that does not invalidate its credentials as
science, within the terms of that genre.

In conclusion

Many aspects of Parmenides's thought remain puzzling even when
we have collected all the scraps of evidence from his own writings
and those of later thinkers who discussed his views. But his
immense significance in philosophical terms has never been
obscured by the difficulties in the nitty-gritty of interpretation. For
one thing, it is obvious that Parmenides throws at us the challenge
of whether we should trust our reason or our senses, in
circumstances when they seem to conflict. Can it ever make sense
to say 'I can see that logically what you say must be right; but I
disagree'? Parmenides's contemporaries probably did not yet see
that a proof is a proof, and that if one is to disagree one must
show what is wrong with the proof, but Parmenides himself asked

us, for the first time as far as we know, to 'judge by reason' (fragment 7.5). And he drew attention to the fact that if his conclusions were true, then the scientific account of the world must be false.

The challenge now, if we think that the world contains things and qualities that vary and change, is to undo Parmenides's argument in the Way of Truth and work out what can be done to preserve some reality for our own mixed-up world. Was Parmenides misled by the slippery language of 'being' and the tricky logic of the word 'not'? If so, how would we need to sharpen up those concepts in order to avoid the pitfalls? Or is there some truth to Parmenides's suggestion that human beings divide up the world according to concepts and

12. Parmenides describes two or three alternative routes of enquiry, only one of which is the correct road that tracks the truth. Another one, followed by ordinary mortals, is 'backward turning', and they wander on it with two heads, perhaps because they try to look two ways at once as they say that reality both is and is not. Fragments 2 and 6 imply that there is also a third wrong way, on which the only thing to say is 'it is not'. Could we actually think about or identify the thing of which we can say only 'it is not'?

distinctions that are mere convention? Do we impose meanings that are not there in reality?

Besides the importance of Parmenides's invention of strict argument as the basis of philosophical enquiry, he is also important for his powerful distinction between appearance and reality. That was a distinction already noticed by Xenophanes, as we shall see in Chapter 4. But it was made more compelling by Parmenides's radically controversial thesis about 'reality'. The appearance/reality distinction is vital for progress in philosophy more generally, since it helps us to see that there might be truths that no one knows. And there may be beliefs that are universally held but actually false. It also shows that science does not proceed by observation, as one might have thought. Observation can only ever provide the untested appearance. In reality, science always advances by mathematical and logical reasoning which deduces how some putative observations are to be systematically explained and adjusted, so as to make sense within a theory amenable to reason.

Parmenides did for science what Plato would later do for morality and aesthetics as well: he alerts us to the fact that opinions are just opinions, and they may differ widely. There may yet be a single truth, which need not be as anyone thought. To search for knowledge is to search for access to the truth, not to collect other people's opinions, and philosophy conducts its unrelenting search for truth in the steps of Parmenides, by respecting sound and rigorous logical argument rather than the variegated tapestry of unexamined opinions.

Chapter 3
Zeno's tortoise

Parmenides started the poem we examined in the last chapter with a vivid description of a young man's mythical journey by chariot to visit a goddess beyond the gates of day and night; yet the goddess in the poem, when the young man gets to see her, persuades him that locomotion is ruled out, along with all other kinds of change, in a universe in which nothing ever comes or goes. Parmenides himself seems not to have taken the message to heart, or at least not so far as to omit the chariot journey from the start of his narrative.

Can we or can we not move from one place to another? Usually we think that we can, and often do. But Parmenides starts a trend in his home town of Elea, and his fellow citizen Zeno is the one who takes up the theme. Zeno has the same bizarre message: nothing moves, all is one. But his great innovation, for which he is justly famous, lies in how he persuades us to accept these unwelcome revisions to our standard beliefs. 'Zeno's paradoxes', as we generally call them, are vivid pieces of thought-experiment which work by setting up a scenario that seems familiar, only to show that things cannot possibly happen as we generally believe them to happen.

Take Achilles and the tortoise, Zeno's best-loved paradox.

Paradox B: Achilles and the tortoise

Achilles, set to compete in the foot-race with his mobility-challenged companion, grants the tortoise something of a head start: when Achilles leaves his starting line the tortoise is already some distance ahead, and it will take Achilles some time, not very long perhaps, to reach the point from which the tortoise is starting out. Surely, we might think, Achilles, swiftest runner in the Greek expedition to Troy, will not remain behind for too much longer:

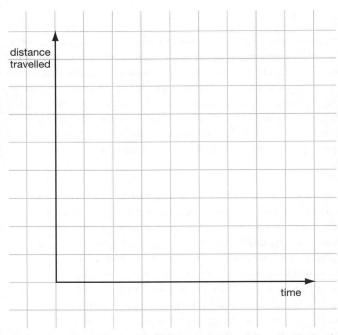

13. Try plotting the distance travelled against time taken on this graph, choosing any speeds you like so long as that of Achilles is faster than that of the tortoise and the tortoise starts somewhere above zero on the distance scale when the time is zero. You will need to enter suitable scales on the vertical and horizontal axes. Where the lines cross, Achilles overtakes the tortoise. How did he do that exactly?

however short the race and however generous the head start, Achilles must reach the finishing line ahead. Not so, in fact. For it takes Achilles a little while to reach the place where the tortoise was allowed to start, and during that time the tortoise, grimly plodding along, has advanced a bit. By the time Achilles gets there, the tortoise is ahead. So Achilles sets out for where the tortoise now is, and it takes him a little while to get there. Sure enough, in that time the tortoise has plodded on, and is again a little further ahead. So Achilles continues, hot on the heels of the tortoise, but by the time he gets to where the tortoise was, the tortoise has moved forward yet again, and Achilles still has not caught up. Now this goes on for ever, since it will always take Achilles some time to cover the distance between himself and the tortoise, and however slowly the tortoise is going he will cover some ground in that time and will no longer be at the previous point but somewhere further ahead. So after all, no matter how long we continue the series, Achilles will never catch up with, let alone overtake, the tortoise, who must surely still be ahead when the race is eventually called off due to bad light.

So much for what we thought we believed: a *paradox* is something which turns out rather contrary to what we expected.

This famous paradox is similar to, but slightly more complex than, another one which aims to show not just that we can't catch up with a slower runner, but that we can't run across the athletics stadium at all. Consider this:

Paradox A: the dichotomy

If you run from A to B you must pass through the halfway point before you get to B. After that halfway point, you will pass another, three-quarters of the way to B. Halfway between that point and B there is another halfway point which you must reach before B. And indeed there are an infinite number of halfway points before you get to B. So you will never reach B itself, since every time you traverse

A ————————————————————— B

14. 'Dichotomy' means cutting in half. Try cutting the line in half repeatedly, by marking points on it as Zeno suggests. How would these cuts relate to actual steps taken by a real runner on a race track? Would the necessity of passing all these places delay him getting to B?

one of the decreasing distances to the next halfway point, there is still an equal distance remaining to be covered, and that distance never becomes nothing. There will always be some gap between you and the end of the journey, so that it is impossible to reach the end. That is, supposing you could ever get started . . . But how could you ever get started? For before reaching the halfway point to B, you must go a quarter of the way; and before going a quarter of the way you must go an eighth of the way, and before that a sixteenth of the way; and so on ad infinitum. *There is no first move to make, for before that there will always be a previous one, which you must have made first. Alas, even the athletes among us will find ourselves permanently paralysed at A.*

The conclusions of Zeno's two paradoxes seem absurd, and this is obviously part of the point. If we can't accept the conclusion, we shall have to reject something else, one of the assumptions that led to the conclusion, and if we do this then the argument follows the pattern that we have learnt to call *reductio ad absurdum*, a pattern of argument which Zeno seems to have perfected. It works by showing that if you accept some hypothesis (which is to be disproved), then an absurd and unacceptable result follows; the best way to escape the absurdity is to deny the hypothesis you started with.

So now let us ask what exactly Zeno thinks is wrong in paradoxes A and B. On one interpretation they are designed to persuade us that motion is impossible: that is, we have to *accept* the apparently absurd conclusion that we can never move from point A. This is because, after all, there is no motion. Parmenides had already made one attempt to persuade us of that, and Zeno's paradoxes about motion are often taken to be further attempts to draw the same conclusion.

Still, if that is the purpose of the paradoxes, notice that they are not structured as a *reductio ad absurdum*. With a *reductio ad absurdum* we should be compelled to *reject* the absurd conclusion, and therefore to question the soundness of the premises from which it was derived, rather than accepting the premises and swallowing the conclusion. So let us think again about the two paradoxes above. Suppose we refuse to swallow the absurd conclusion: suppose we say it can't be true that Achilles never overtakes the tortoise; and it can't be true that the runner never gets to the end of the racecourse. What then? We shall have to reject some assumption that got the argument to that conclusion. But which assumption are we to reject?

There may be two answers to this question. One will be the answer that Zeno hopes we shall give. He must have produced the arguments to persuade us to change our views, and there will be a specific target that he had in mind. We can ask, historically, what that target was, and, philosophically, whether we are obliged to agree with Zeno and revise our view of the world. The other answer will be the answer that a modern mathematician might offer, in order to escape the absurd conclusion. The mathematician might think that Zeno's paradox only gets going because he has missed some obvious truth in mathematics, and hence that we need not, after all, target the assumption that Zeno himself had hoped we should target.

Both these questions are still hotly debated, and there is scope for you to explore your own solutions. I shall make one possible suggestion on each front. On the first question, 'what did Zeno mean us to throw out?', some scholars have suggested that the target was infinite division of time and space. We can be pretty sure that Zeno was interested in proving that plurality is impossible; he follows Parmenides in holding that there cannot be more than one thing in the world. In these two paradoxes he generates a bizarre result by building in the idea that however small a part of time or space you take, you can always divide it yet more finely. No matter how near to the end of the racecourse the runner gets, there is always another half distance to go, and that too can be divided into two tasks, and so on. Because the series of divisions, cutting the remaining space in half, goes on *ad infinitum* there can never be a last step in the series. There can be no move that finally crosses the divide and reaches the end. This is true, and it follows from taking space to be a continuum, divisible conceptually to infinity. Typically we do hold nowadays that space (mathematically) is a continuum, even though physically it is hard to draw lines or points that don't get on top of each other (but that is a fault of the thickness of our pencils – in mathematical theory there is no limit to how many cuts we can make on a finite line). It is that assumption that generates the impossibility of completing the journey across the racetrack, because there is no last task. So perhaps Zeno meant us to conclude that infinite divisions of space are impossible.

If that is so, we can see that Paradox B takes the same issue one step further. Opponents since Aristotle (see Box 10) have often pointed out that the puzzle in Paradox A can be resolved if we accept that time too is infinitely divisible, in exactly the same way as space is. But Paradox B shows that this is no easy answer, for in that paradox we are assuming that time, as well as space, is infinitely divisible: that is how the paradox gets going. However short a time it takes Achilles to traverse the distance between himself and the tortoise, that time is still a portion of time and it will be long enough for the tortoise to have moved. There never comes a point at which time runs out: we can always subdivide it and find that the tortoise has a

> Zeno's argument assumes that it is impossible to traverse an
> infinite number of things, or to touch an infinite number of
> things individually, in a finite time. But this is false. For both
> lengths and times – and indeed all *continua* – are said to be
> infinite in two ways: either by division or in respect of their
> extremities. Now it is not possible to touch a quantitatively
> infinite number of things in a finite time, but it *is* possible so
> to touch things infinite by division. For time itself is infinite
> in this way. Hence it follows that what is infinite is traversed
> in an infinite and not in a finite time, and that the infinite
> things are touched at infinitely not at finitely many instants.
>
> Box 10: Aristotle (384–322 BC) responds to Zeno's paradox
> with an analysis of two kinds of infinity, *Physics* 233a, 21–31
> (tr. J. Barnes).

moment to get ahead again. In this way it makes sense to see
Paradox A as the simpler and Paradox B as the more complex in a
pair of arguments to show that absurdity follows from the infinite
division of space and time.

Exploring the answer to the second question, 'how might a
mathematician try to resolve the absurdity?', we can appeal again to
Aristotle's observation (in Box 10) that the infinite divisions within
a finite whole do not make the whole any larger than it was: a finite
whole infinitely divided still makes a finite whole. So the distance
from A to B in Paradox A remains a finite distance and can be
traversed in a finite time, no matter how finely we subdivide it. For
each distance in the decreasing series takes the runner a shorter
time to complete, and as the distances get vanishingly small, so the
time taken to pass through them becomes vanishingly small; in
both cases the sum of the whole set of parts, if we add them all up,
turns out to be the whole that we started with before we divided it.
Mathematics has techniques for calculating the sum of an infinite

series, but the simplest proof is simply to picture the problem spatially. In dividing the distance A to B in Figure 14, we are always subdividing *between* the limits at A and B, and the total of all the parts added up will clearly be the length of the line from A to B. Cashing this geometry out in terms of movement, we realize that the runner does not after all have an infinite distance to cover but a finite one, and he completes his diminishing tasks ever more quickly as long as he maintains a constant speed.

This fact is not quite so clear in Paradox B, since we don't know in advance the finite distance from Achilles's starting point, nor could we predict the point at which he would overtake the tortoise: point B, if you like, does not appear on the drawing *until* Achilles gets there (and finds the tortoise already there). Nevertheless if you completed your graph in Figure 13 you will have discovered where that point is for your pair of competitors. It is the point at which their lines cross. Between where Achilles starts and that passing point there is a finite distance and a finite time. Zeno's paradox works by persistently subdividing to make smaller and smaller divisions *within* the limited portion of time and space between the beginning of the race and the moment when Achilles coincides with the tortoise, immediately before he gets ahead. At the *end* of that portion of the race, there is after all a passing point, and we can calculate when it occurs.

So mathematics can provide proofs that certain kinds of infinite series tending towards zero have a finite sum, and that Zeno's paradoxes appeal to series of that kind. Because the sum of the parts is finite, and the rate of progress constant, the time taken to complete the task must be finite. So the paradoxes don't work.

But is this really a solution? It shows us what we knew already, that the distance from A to B is finite, and that the infinite division subdivides a finite quantity. What it does not show us is how we can complete the task, since it does not avoid the challenge that there is no last move, no move that crosses the boundary from 'not yet there' to 'there now'. If the series is genuinely infinite, then mathematically there will be no point that is the last point before reaching B, and no time at which Achilles changes from being behind the tortoise to being level with her. There is a time at which he is not yet there, and there is a time at which he is already there, but no time at which he exchanges the former description for the latter. This is a counter-intuitive observation. Mathematicians evade the difficulty by the use of the fiction of 'infinitesimal' quantities, which treat the series as if it effectively had a last member, of infinitesimal size. But the fact remains that in reality the parts do not suddenly become 'infinitesimally small' as though that were some ultimate size; in fact they go on becoming ever smaller *ad infinitum*. So Zeno was right, and we cannot evade the truth that the completion of the task may come *between* two identifiable points in time and space but not *at* any time or place. Additionally, there is an unavoidable vagueness about how far apart such identifiable points will need to be.

Zeno's worries about locations in space and time emerge again in other evidence from later authors. Some key examples are shown in Box 11. We can see a common thread running through his work: first, his method of pressing ordinary assumptions about physics until they yield metaphysical nonsense; second, his penchant for infinite series; third, his interest in parts (of bodies, space, or time) with or without extension; and fourth, his interest in the analysis of motion from place to place, and how it can be measured. Notice the reference to the moving arrow in Box 11: Zeno may have suggested that we might try to measure the arrow's progress by whether it is adjacent to something of equal size to itself; the place it occupies will not do, however, as a measure against which to plot its progress, since it is *always* in a place its own size. It never moves beyond its own place, and hence, by that criterion of rest, appears to be still for the whole period of its travel. This generates what we know as Zeno's third paradox. In a fourth paradox, rather confusingly presented in the sources, he seems also to have shown that it is equally impossible to measure motion against other

> **Zeno abolishes motion, saying: 'The moving object moves neither in the place in which it is nor in a place in which it isn't.'**
>
> **(Diogenes Laertius, 9.72)**
>
> **Zeno's puzzle seeks an explanation: for if every thing is in a place, evidently there will be a place of place, and so on ad infinitum.**
>
> **(Aristotle, *Physics*, 209a23)**
>
> **Zeno commits a fallacy: 'For if each thing is invariably at rest when adjacent to what is equal' he says, 'and the moving object is invariably in the present, then the moving arrow is immobile.'**
>
> **(Aristotle, *Physics*, 239b5)**
>
> Box 11: Responses to Zeno's views on space and time.

similar bodies stationed alongside the body whose motion is to be measured.

Whether or not Zeno was merely trying to defend Parmenides from the ridicule of others, there is no doubt that he has pushed the analysis of reality onto a new plane. He makes us think not just about objects in space, but about space as a structure within which they exist; about motion not just as the behaviour of physical bodies, but as a theoretical concept involving conceptual divisions in space and time; about number not just as a way of counting finite bodies but as a rational system potentially (or actually) continuing *ad infinitum,* with the problematic consequences that that might entail; about the notions of 'before' and 'after' in time, and how long the duration of the present is. These topics belong to what we call metaphysics, and Zeno's puzzles enter territory that is still fought over.

Chapter 4

Reality and appearance: more adventures in metaphysics

It would be difficult to outdo Zeno as a master of striking images designed to make us think twice or three times about the nature of reality. But he is not alone. Other Presocratic philosophers deserve to be mentioned alongside him, philosophers who, like Zeno, suggested that reality and appearance can be prised apart and that the nature of reality may not be entirely obvious.

Xenophanes of Colophon: the invention of monotheism

First, and pre-eminent because of his staggeringly early date, is Xenophanes, born perhaps a hundred years before Zeno. Xenophanes wrote in verse – typically, for this was the standard way to publish at the time – and he was a man of many interests. Only some of his poems are on philosophical themes.

As we discovered in the last chapter, it was Zeno who invented the strict form of *reductio ad absurdum*. But long before Zeno, Xenophanes had come up with a similar method to cast doubt on the conventional notions of the gods. Reconstructing from the material provided by Clement of Alexandria (in Box 12), we can see that Xenophanes wanted to propose philosophical monotheism: the existence of one all-powerful and all-knowing god who has no

Instructing us that God is one and bodiless, Xenophanes of Colophon offers the following:

(a) 'One god, greatest among gods and humans,
   like mortals neither in form nor in thought.'
   And again:

(b) 'But mortals think that the gods are born
   and have the mortals' own clothes and voice and form'
   And again:

(c) 'But if cows and horses or lions had hands
   or could draw with their hands and make artefacts like men make
   horses would draw the forms of their gods like horses, cows like cows,
   and make their bodies such as the form they each had themselves.'
   (Clement of Alexandria, *Miscellanies* 5.14.109.1–3,
   quoting fragments 23, 14, and 15)

(d) As Xenophanes of Colophon says, the Ethiopians making them snub nosed and dark, and the Thracians making them blue eyed and red-haired . . .
   (Clement of Alexandria, *Miscellanies* 7.22,
   identified as fragment 16)

Box 12: Xenophanes argues that traditional images of the gods have no basis.

visible form and engages in no physical activity. Xenophanes is, apparently, the first of many distinguished philosophers in the Western world to take this line.

15. Bendis, originally a Thracian divinity, appears here on an Athenian vase, accompanied by a doe and wearing exotic Thracian costume to mark her foreign status.

Clement starts by quoting fragment 23 (quote (a) in Box 12). In these lines Xenophanes actually asserts his own view about god. But in the next quotation he goes on to criticize the typical gods of his day, by an argument that attempts to reduce them to absurdity. First, he points out (fragment 14, quote (b) in Box 12) that people think of their gods as similar to themselves, having the clothes and features they have themselves. In quote (d), taken from a different part of Clement's work, we can find a further step in the argument. Often identified as fragment 16, it points out that people of different races and ethnic groups picture the gods in their own image: black people have black-skinned gods, the red-haired Thracians have red-haired gods. Finally, Xenophanes extrapolates, in quote (c): isn't it obvious that animals too would simply draw their own gods like themselves, if they could draw?

By taking us on a cumulative sequence from our own familiar gods, through those of other ethnic groups, to those of animals, Xenophanes shows that our own images have no more authority than those of animals. There is probably also supposed to be an intrinsic absurdity in the idea that animals could be right about the

16. On Athenian black-figure vases, the painting is in black on an orange background, so all the characters have black faces; but here the painter Exekias has clearly distinguished the Greek warrior in the centre, whose lightly coloured flowing locks hang below his helmet, from the two recognizably black squires on either side, with their dark curly hair, snub noses, and convincingly black faces. The features are those noted by Xenophanes as typical for Ethiopians – and their gods – in fragment 16.

gods, or that gods could think and behave like horses and cows. When we invent gods like ourselves, Xenophanes suggests, we are just doing what irrational animals do. So our gods are no better than cow gods.

This method of argument is similar to, though less sophisticated than, Zeno's *reductio ad absurdum*. Zeno argued for an unchanging unity by discrediting the common idea of a plurality of things. Similarly, Xenophanes discredits pluralistic religion and its varied anthropomorphic gods, in order to promote his new theory that the godhead must be an unchanging unity.

17. As trade and travel became common, the Greeks observed that other cultures had different kinds of gods. In Egypt the gods had long been pictured as animals. This Egyptian fertility goddess dates from the century before Xenophanes was born. Would this counter-example to the idea that we all create our gods in our own image be difficult for Xenophanes to accommodate?

But can we know?

Xenophanes is also justly famous for another 'first': sceptical doubts about whether human beings really know anything. The richest text is fragment 34, in Box 13. The overall gist of this passage is, as Sextus Empiricus remarks, to deny that any human being genuinely has knowledge. But we might feel that Sextus has slightly overstated the case. Is everything literally *unknowable*? In lines 1 to 2, Xenophanes says that no one is actually in a position to know, but it is not clear what the range of things is that he means we can't know. Notice that line 2 mentions the gods. That might be one difficulty: we can't know about the gods perhaps. But then it mentions the things Xenophanes has to say about 'everything'. Unfortunately, we cannot be sure whether this 'everything' means all subjects in general or just the subjects Xenophanes was writing about in his book. And since we don't have his book, we don't know the range of subjects that would include.

Furthermore, we might notice that the comments in lines 1 to 2 are about 'men'. Humans may not be in a position to know some things,

---

Xenophanes . . . says that everything is unknowable, when he writes:

'And the clear truth no man has seen nor will there be anyone in a position of knowing concerning the gods and the things I say about everything:

for even if he hit the mark, saying things that are spot on the truth,

yet still he does not himself know; but belief extends across all.'

Sextus Empiricus, *Adv Math*, 7.49, quoting Xenophanes, fragment 34

Box 13: Getting things right is not the same as knowing.

---

but it does not follow that the things are really *unknowable* and could not be known to someone ideally situated, say the all-seeing god whom Xenophanes described in other parts of his poem.

Xenophanes continues, in line 3 of fragment 34, to draw a distinction between saying something that just happens to be true and knowing it. This is an exciting moment in philosophy, since it starts the search for what makes the difference between true belief and knowledge. The project has occupied philosophers ever since Xenophanes drew the distinction here. Of course, to know something is to have a *true* belief, not a false one, but as Xenophanes points out in line 3, you can hit the mark spot on and not know it. What else is required to count as knowing? Xenophanes does not say what it is, but he does say that what we humans have, even when we get the answer right, is only the belief. We don't actually *know* that we've got it right.

Why is Xenophanes so sceptical that anyone ever actually *knows*? One possibility is that the word translated as 'the clear truth' in line 1 refers to something special, something that is not superficially and immediately apparent. Maybe we have access to how things appear on the surface: that sort of thing people *can* see. But suppose the appearances do not completely or precisely match up with how things really are. The reality may be something deeper, something which we are not well placed to know about, just by looking at things from our perspective. So Xenophanes might be saying that we have only superficial understanding, and we never get to knowledge of the *clear truth*.

Appearance and reality

How we are placed can indeed affect how things seem, and Xenophanes was aware of that. 'If god had not made yellow honey,' he is reported to have said, 'they would say that the fig was far sweeter.' In other words, we would not be well placed to judge the sweetness of figs on an accurate scale, if we had no experience of the greater sweetness of honey. We would overestimate figs, taking them to be the sweetest thing there is. But then how can we be well placed to judge how sweet *honey* is, given that there may be yet sweeter things we have yet to encounter or might never in our lives encounter? The Greeks of Xenophanes's day had, of course, never tasted cane sugar, which reached the old world from America only in recent times.

We have met the distinction between appearance and reality already in dealing with Parmenides in Chapter 2. But now we see that before Parmenides, Xenophanes had already entered caveats about human knowledge which invoke the idea of a truth not apparent to perception, a truth which we may never discover by merely investigating how things appear.

The distinction between knowledge and belief is a theme that continues throughout Greek philosophy, emerging crucially in the central works of Plato. In Plato it recurs together with the idea, hinted at here in Xenophanes and taken to extremes in Parmenides and Zeno, that there may be a problem about the relation between physical objects as they seem to be and the metaphysical reality as it really is.

Distrusting the senses: how can we be sure?

Besides Xenophanes, we should also juxtapose with Zeno three other Presocratics of Zeno's day or a bit after, who, like Zeno, explored the distinction between appearance and reality. These are Melissus, Anaxagoras, and Democritus. The latter two also shared Zeno's interest in things very small.

Melissus, though he came from the island of Samos on the other side of the Greek world, is often classified as an honorary 'Eleatic' with Parmenides and Zeno. This is because of his commitment to roughly similar, and equally counter-intuitive, views. Melissus was a monist, like Parmenides, and held that plurality was an illusion. That led him to the idea that the senses must deliver a misleading message.

Suppose that we receive two conflicting messages. The senses indicate that many things exist; reason insists that only one can be real. Which we should trust and which we should reject? Melissus raises this question and decides against the senses, in the passage known as fragment 8, part of which is shown in Box 14.

Melissus notes a conflict between reason and sense in the sentence numbered (4) in Box 14. He had already tried to prove by reasoned argument that reality must be unique, eternal, unchanging, and infinite. Here, in fragment 8, he suggests that evidence acquired through sight, hearing, and so on suggests otherwise; the senses suggest that there are many different things and that they change. So much the worse for sight and hearing, in Melissus's view.

Melissus appears to grant, in sentence (1), that there could indeed be several things, but he thinks that we must be wrong about them changing. Hence he concludes, in the sentence marked (6), 'So it is clear that we do not see correctly'.

Given a conflict between reason and sense, why should we infer at once that sense must be wrong? Notice the use of the word 'seem' in sentence (6). We are quite used to the idea that things can *seem* otherwise than they are; the way something appears is not necessarily how it is. Hence there is no major crisis in language if we conclude that some appearances are deceptive or subject to correction. But it will be inferences based on reason that lead us to correct or question the inferences that were based on perception. When the sun appears to sink behind the western hills in the evening, we often talk of it 'going down'. Yet once we have been persuaded by the proofs of mathematical astronomy, we readily

(1) If there existed many things, they would have to be such as
I say the one thing is . . . (2) Each of them must always be just
what it is . . . (3) But what is hot seems to us to become cold,
and what is cold hot . . . (4) Now these things do not agree
with one another. (5) For we said that there are many eternal
things with forms and strengths of their own, but they all
seem to us to alter and to change from what they were each
time they were seen. (6) So it is clear that we do not see
correctly, nor is it accurate the way those many things seem
to be. (7) For they would not change if they were true, but
each would be as it seemed to be; for nothing is stronger than
what is true. (8) And if they changed, what exists would have
perished and what does not exist would have come into
being. (9) In this way, then, if there exist many things, they
must be such as the one thing is.

> Extracts from Melissus, fragment 8,
> taken from Simplicius, *In de caelo*, 558–9
> (tr. J. Barnes, with alterations)

Box 14: Melissus on the contradiction between sense and reason.

concede that relative to us the sun is actually stationary, and it is we
who have moved round. We may still *feel* as if we are at rest
watching a moving object out there, but those appearances can be
over-ridden by our greater trust in theory.

So it sounds natural to say that the senses occasionally give a
false impression. It makes sense to think, 'It looked as though it
was sinking, but it was really staying put'. Can we then move swiftly,
as Melissus does in fragment 8, to claim that *all* that we see or
hear is invariably wrong, since the *whole lot* conflicts with a proof
based on reason? Where exactly would that proof come from, if
there is *nothing* we can rely on from the senses?

Let's look at what Melissus offers in the rest of the material in Box 14. His argument relies on certain claims about what it is to 'exist' or to 'be true'. 'For they would not change if they were true' says Melissus in sentence (7) of fragment 8. Here he uses 'true' in a traditional sense that has become rather unfamiliar in modern philosophy. It conveys the idea that something is genuine, accurate, and sound. Here it is used of things: something is 'true' if it really exists according to the way something ought to exist if it is really real or truly there, and properly corresponds with how we believe it to be. 'Nothing is stronger than what is true' then ascribes to reality the strength to outdo what is unreal and merely an appearance, and hence to exist more permanently than the changeable things that we seem to see.

In this way Melissus seems to infer that what really exists must be permanent and immutable, because it is too tough to pass away, and all change involves the destruction of a previous state of being. The argument depends upon investigating what we mean by saying something is real or exists. Permanence, Melissus suggests, is part of the concept of truth or existence. Is that so? How would we check up?

Even if Melissus's analysis of the concept of existence is faulty, his procedure is very interesting. He challenges the data of sense experience by appealing to conceptual truths, facts about what a certain predicate (here 'true') must entail. These facts seem to escape the need to appeal to sense experience. We check up what is true about being true by examining our notion of being true, not by checking any things in the external world. So the argument seems to find a way of challenging the value of sense experience without begging the question. Melissus casts doubt on the senses by privileging the logical grammar of the word 'true'. But, we might ask, did we learn how to use the word 'true' without relying on the senses?

Anaxagoras of Clazomenae and Democritus of Abdera: minute bits of this and that

Besides Melissus, two other thinkers appealed to the idea that there was a true reality that differed fundamentally from the superficial appearances: Anaxagoras and Democritus. Both suggested that reality was hidden because it involved components too small or too mixed-up for us to see.

For Democritus, macroscopic objects were composed of microscopic atoms: 'atoms', meaning 'uncuttable', because they could not be divided. In principle, according to Democritus, we could explain all the behaviour of ordinary things in the world by the movement of the atoms. The atoms themselves never alter their own characteristics. They just rearrange themselves into various collections.

In a similar way Anaxagoras had earlier suggested that there must be hidden substances and qualities in things we encounter around us. Processes like nutrition and evaporation, for instance, make it seem as if one thing can change into another. We eat meat and our hair grows. So how did the hair-like matter come from the meat, which doesn't appear to be made of hair? The fact is, Anaxagoras explained, the food we eat, no matter what it is, invariably contains small quantities of the right sort of matter to account for what happens to it once we've eaten it. Indeed (in a fit of generosity rather beyond the strict requirements of chemistry and physics), Anaxagoras guarantees that *everything* contains some of *everything*, so *anything could in theory change into anything*.

Both Democritus and Anaxagoras suggested that explanations could be found in the nature of the matter out of which things are made. These explanations would theoretically be available, if we were in a position to calculate exactly what the structure of the material is really like. But neither thought that the explanation could be completed in practice. The limit of comprehension is due not just to their lack of electron microscopes or other instruments for detecting very small particles; for even if we saw to a level below that visible to the naked eye, the need for explanation would not come to an end.

The endless sequence of explanation is explicit in Anaxagoras. Even the ingredients that go to make up something and account for its behaviour are themselves composed of ingredients which are themselves again composed of ingredients, as Simplicius explains in the first text in Box 15. In every case, behaviour is a consequence of both the predominant features (which make it seem to be such and such) and also the hidden features (which can make it do otherwise inexplicable things). And this dual explanation will apply as much to the hidden ingredients as to the macroscopic items we encounter in daily life.

But still it remains true for Anaxagoras that in principle the material composition (if we could know it in detail) would account for the current behaviour of each item in the world. Unless the thing is alive, that is. For living things, it looks as though the explanation must be supplemented by appeal to another principle, what Anaxagoras called 'Mind' (see Box 16).

In Democritus it is less obvious that explanation will go on *ad infinitum*, since the theory posits ultimate particles that cannot physically decompose into further elements. Yet the end of explanation is an illusion even here, since the behaviour of each atom will reflect its internal structure: perhaps its size and shape, the angles of its curves and points, the smoothness of its surfaces, the hardness of its core. (These are suggestions – see if you can work out from the text in Box 17 what physical properties an atom might have in itself, according to Democritus.)

At the very beginning of his book, Anaxagoras says that things were infinite: 'Together were all things, infinite both in quantity and in smallness.' Among the principles there is neither a smallest nor a largest: 'For of the small,' he says, 'there is no smallest, but there is always a smaller. For what is cannot not be. And again compared with the large there is always a larger, and it is equal to the small in quantity. But compared with itself each thing is both large and small.' For if everything is in everything, and everything is extracted from everything, then from what is taken to be the smallest thing something smaller will be extracted, and what is taken to be the largest has been extracted from something larger than itself.

Simplicius, *Commentary on the Physics*, 164,
quoting texts known as fragments 1 and 3
(tr. J. Barnes, altered)

The distinguished natural scientist Anaxagoras, attacking the senses for their weakness, says 'We are not capable of discerning the truth by reason of their feebleness,' and he offers as proof of their untrustworthiness the gradual change of colours. For if we take two colours, black and white, and then pour from one to the other drop by drop, our sight will not be able to distinguish the gradual changes even though they exist in nature.

Sextus Empiricus, *Against the Mathematicians*, VII 90,
quoting the text known as fragment 21 (tr. J. Barnes)

Box 15: Anaxagoras on the infinitely small.

> Mind is something infinite and self-controlling, and it has been mixed with no thing but is alone itself by itself. For if it were not by itself but had been mixed with some other thing, it would share in all things if it had been mixed with any. For in everything there is a share of everything, as I have said earlier, and the things commingled with it would have prevented it from controlling anything in the way in which it does when it is actually alone by itself. For it is the finest of all things and the purest, and it possesses all knowledge about everything, and it has the greatest strength. And mind controls all those things, both great and small, which possess soul.
>
> Anaxagoras, fragment 12 (tr. J. Barnes)

Box 16: Anaxagoras's Mind: is he talking about our minds or some super-cosmic mind?

Even if these features are not separable from the whole, they are explanations that appeal to features at the sub-atomic level. So suppose we could see the atoms under magnification? Would that tell us some final answer and call a halt to the search for explanation? Of course not, for we should see only how the atoms *appear,* and how they *appear* to behave. We should still not see what lay below the superficial appearance and explained *why* they look like that or what accounts for them appearing to behave like that.

Both Democritus and Anaxagoras try to explain the puzzling behaviour of ordinary reality by appeal to a microscopic replica of reality, in which another set of tiny bodies or minute scraps of stuff move around and cause things to happen. As a way to overcome the difficulty of explaining changes in the world, this ultimately emerges as unsatisfying: if there were problems with explaining chemical and physical events as they appear to us, there will be the

18. Democritus became known to later tradition as the 'laughing philosopher', largely as a result of the circulation of apocryphal stories about his cheerful attitude to life and fortune, and his perception of the follies of other men.

same problems with explaining the reactions between smaller and yet smaller bodies. There will be another appearance and reality divide at the next level down, and it will be necessary to appeal yet again to deeper phenomena to explain the apparent behaviour of the first set of hypothetical particles, and so on *ad infinitum*.

Twenty-first century science meets the same difficulty. It continues

> Democritus thinks that the nature of eternal things consists in small substances, infinite in quantity, and for them he posits a place, distinct from them and infinite in extent. He calls place by the names 'void', 'nothing' and 'infinite'; and each of the substances he calls 'thing', 'solid' and 'being'. He thinks that the substances are so small that they escape our senses, and that they possess all sorts of forms and all sorts of shapes and differences in magnitude. . . . He explains how the substances remain together in terms of the way in which the bodies entangle with and get hold of one another; for some of them are uneven, some hooked, some concave, some convex, and others have innumerable other differences.
>
> Aristotle, *On Democritus*, from a quotation in Simplicius's commentary on the *De Caelo*, 294, tr. J. Barnes

Box 17: Democritus and the properties of atoms. What features does an individual atom have, as opposed to a collection of atoms?

to pursue quantum physics in the search for explanations of phenomena at the atomic level, which were themselves intended to explain phenomena at the level of experience. But so long as the explanations remain of the same order as the phenomena to be explained (physics explained by physics, mathematics explained by mathematics), the same demand for explanation will simply emerge again at the next level. Democritus's atoms provided inspiration to Robert Boyle and others when they rediscovered his ideas in the 17th century; but the atomic theory was destined never to escape from the dilemma of unending gaps in explanation.

Philosophy, meanwhile, had continued to probe the appearance and reality distinction for other riches.

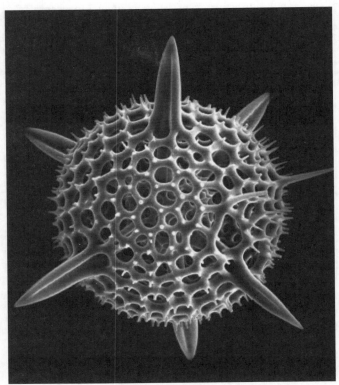

19. An image of the fossilized shell of a microscopic ocean animal, created by an electron microscope. When we see something in the normal way, we are actually detecting the effects of photons reflected by objects. In an analogous way, the electron microscope creates its image by picking up a pattern of even smaller particles, this time electrons. It then converts the data into a visible image of a size large enough for us to view by means of reflected light. It gives us an indirect route to discovering that there is a beautiful world of tiny objects too small for our senses to detect. But is there still an appearance-reality gap, between the image and what it is of? If so, should it worry us?

Other worlds

Xenophanes, Parmenides, Zeno, Melissus, Anaxagoras, and Democritus: all these thinkers have been feeling their way first to the primitive idea that what we find out with our senses may be unreliable, and then to the idea that it will always need to be tested against reason and theory. That scepticism is, of course, shared by any modern scientist, who will always establish controlled experiments designed to isolate problems caused by observational deficiencies and misleading results. But beyond that lies the more ambitious claim, that observation might be systematically misleading, and indeed that the *entire* material world might be flawed and unreliable.

This tempting thought can feed on a number of features of human experience: it warms to the idea that there are immortal gods who are wiser, more permanent, and less visible than the mere mortals who wander the world we know; it feeds upon the hope that the human soul might be more lasting than the body; and it grounds the conviction that truth and goodness remain the same for all eternity, even when the world is full of evil and suffering, and corruption is rife among mortal powers. It is true that Democritus, the latest of our thinkers, was later to inspire in Epicurus the least other-worldly of all philosophies. But before that, the impulse to divide the world of real being from the world of appearances had taken deeper root, blossoming in the 4th century BC into the 'other worldliness' of Plato.

Plato's metaphysics grew out of that of Parmenides, together with a strong feel for Heraclitus's account of the physical world as a world of incessant change. His ethics were deeply inspired by Socrates, but his views on the soul also pick up on motifs that emerge in Pythagoras, to whom we shall turn in Chapter 6. The world has never forgotten Plato, but it is worthwhile to see the extent of his legacy from the great minds of Presocratic thought, including those pioneers who opened up the territory that would become the theory of knowledge, and explored the metaphysics of appearance and reality.

Chapter 5
Heraclitus

They told me, Heraclitus, they told me you were dead,
They brought me bitter news to hear and bitter tears to shed.
I wept as I remember'd how often you and I
Had tired the sun with talking and sent him down the sky.

William Cory

The Heraclitus of this poem is not our philosopher. He is another Heraclitus, friend of the poet Callimachus (3rd century BC) whose epitaph on the death of his friend has entered the English poetry books via this memorable translation by William Cory (1823–92). Whereas Callimachus looks back on a friend whose conversation and companionship were delightful, those who look back on Heraclitus the philosopher of Ephesus remember only a proud and arrogant man who spoke in riddles; a man who thought no one would be able to understand what he was saying, and who didn't really care. The two epigrams in Box 18 express a common perception of Heraclitus's character.

Yet for all his famous obscurity, Heraclitus has inspired many people to take up the challenge in epigram (ii), and volunteer to be our guide. Who is the initiate who can transform Heraclitus's proverbial obscurity into brilliant enlightenment? Plenty of candidates present themselves in the history of Western philosophy. Some examples of their verdicts appear in Boxes 19 and 20.

(i) Heraclitus I: why drag me up and down, illiterates?

   I laboured not for you, but for those who understand.

   To me, one man is thirty thousand, but the innumerable
      innumerate don't count,

   Not one. These things I proclaim even in the presence of
      Persephone.

(ii) Not so fast, winding up the scroll upon its navel! That
      book,

   Ephesian Heraclitus's: for the path is mighty hard to get
      along;

   Gloom there is, and unenlightened darkness; but should an
      initiate

   Take you in, then it's more brilliant than the unclouded sun.

   Diogenes Laertius, *Lives of the Philosophers*, 9.16

Box 18: Two epigrams on Heraclitus, quoted by Diogenes
Laertius. Can you find witty allusions in both poems to sayings of
Heraclitus quoted in this chapter? Might there be other allusions
to lost sayings that we cannot now identify?

There is no doubt that Heraclitus has seemed both obscure and
deep to generations of thinkers. Yet his sayings, in so far as we can
reconstruct them, provide material for many different versions of
his thought, as Heidegger remarks in passage (ii) of Box 20.

Everyone who reads Heraclitus (or what is left of Heraclitus) finds
his or her own ideas somewhere there. And those who disagree
about what Heraclitus meant can argue – as Aristotle does in
passage (ii) of Box 19, and many others have since then – that what
he seems to say is not what he really meant. But Heidegger's point is
worth taking to heart: Heraclitus speaks variously to various
readers, and even if we had a complete text, there could be no single
definitive interpretation of his 'mysteries'.

(i) Socrates: Those people (materialists) are indeed very splendidly illiterate; but the others, whose mysteries I am about to betray to you, are much more sophisticated. The starting point of these mysteries is one on which all that we previously said also depends, namely that everything is motion and there is nothing else besides that, but there are two kinds of motion . . .

Plato, *Theaetetus*, 156a

(ii) But one could quickly force Heraclitus himself (by questioning him in this way) to admit that contradictory propositions can never be true in the same respect. But as it is he adopted this view because he did not understand the meaning of his own utterance. But if what he said is true, it follows in all circumstances that that very saying is false – namely the claim that the same thing can both be and not be at the same time . . . .

Aristotle, *Metaphysics*, 1062a31–b2

Box 19: Two early guides enlighten us about Heraclitus's real meaning: (i) Socrates in Plato's dialogue *Theaetetus* begins to expound the mysteries of universal motion as taught by Heraclitus, and (ii) Aristotle offers to improve on Heraclitus's own understanding of what he meant by the co-existence of opposites.

A 'very short introduction' to Heraclitus cannot, therefore, be cast as a summary of Heraclitus's real meaning. It will, rather, be a sample of some impossible questions. There seems no better place to start than with Aristotle's puzzle (Box 19) over whether Heraclitus embraced contradiction.

The 'unity of opposites' and the law of non-contradiction

Take the proposition 'water is good for you'. If that proposition is true, then surely it cannot also be true to say that 'water is not good for you'. This so-called 'principle of non-contradiction' is taken by Aristotle (in the *Metaphysics*, from which the passage in Box 19 is taken) to be not just a fundamental law of good reasoning, but also a law of *thought*. That is, Aristotle considered it impossible actually to believe or *think* both of two strictly contradictory propositions.

Yet sometimes we might want to say that water is good for you and it is not good for you. Perhaps it depends on how much water, or when you drink it, or we might have meant to refer to different people by the word 'you', or it might be good to drink but not good for the skin. The two propositions 'water is good for you' and 'water is not good for you' were perhaps incomplete: they *looked* contradictory, but really they referred to different circumstances. A reasonable person could surely assert both, providing they meant slightly different things. Sometimes one might say something quite obvious, but choose to express it in the form of a contradiction just to make it striking.

Was Heraclitus just saying something obvious when he said that opposites were one and the same? Hippolytus lists some quotations which play with contradiction, in the passage shown in Box 21. Hippolytus suggests that Heraclitus was denying the difference between pairs of opposites (particularly ones that typically carry connotations of value), and indeed it is true that, in the quotations he gives, Heraclitus speaks of various apparently contrasted things (day and night, or up and down) being 'one' or 'one and the same'. Yet his point does not seem exactly to be that the opposite qualities themselves are no different, or have no significance, but rather that they can both be used to describe the same thing at the same time.

In the last example in box 21, about the sea water, we see a quite obvious point (that salt water is fine for fish but undrinkable for us) expressed with a bare contradiction as its first phrase: 'The sea water most pure and most impure'. Yet the point is not left as a naked contradiction, any more than the equally true observation that the road up and the road down are one and the same. If there is a general point to be extracted from these sayings in Box 21, it need

Therefore Heraclitus says that neither darkness nor light, neither evil nor good are any different but one and the same. For instance, he upbraids Hesiod on the grounds that he knew day and night; for day and night are one, he says, speaking in this kind of way:

> Teacher of most, Hesiod: him they take to know most, who did not recognise night and day; for they are one.

And good and bad:

> The doctors – says Heraclitus – cutting, burning, torturing the weak viciously in every way, beg fees though they deserve to take none from the sick, producing these same things: goods and illnesses.

And straight and crooked are the same, he says:

> For the fuller's shop – he says – the straight and twisted path – the rotation of the instrument called kochlias in the fuller's shop is straight and twisted, for it goes up and round and round at the same time – is one and the same – he says.

And up and down are one and the same:

> The road up and down is one and the same.

And the impure and the pure are one and the same and the drinkable and the undrinkable are one and the same:

> The sea – he says – water most pure and most impure; for fishes drinkable and healthy; for humans undrinkable and deadly.

Hippolytus, Refutation of all heresies, 9. 10.2–5

Box 21: Hippolytus of Rome quotes evidence for Heraclitus's assimilation of opposites (fragments 57, 58, 59, 60, 61).

20. The way up and the way down is one and the same . . .

not be a unity of opposites (if that means denying the difference between the opposite characteristics). It might be about the fact that opposites arise from someone's viewpoint (for example, purity from the fishes' viewpoint, uphill from the point of view of someone starting up the road). So can anything have one of these characteristics independently of any observer? Surely words like 'up' or 'pure' make sense only in the kind of context where someone needs to draw the contrast for a reason?

Everything flows

Where else in Heraclitus might Aristotle have found something that looked like a worrying form of contradiction? Aristotle seems to think (in the passage quoted in Box 19) that Heraclitus claimed that something can both be and not be at the same time. He may have in mind something like the second saying quoted in Box 22.

The dark Heraclitus . . . uses god-speak of the natural world when he says

> Gods are mortal, humans immortal, living the death of those, dying the life of these.

And again

> Into the same rivers we step in and we don't step in, we are and we are not.

And he allegorises the whole of science in an enigmatic way.
Heraclitus Homericus, *Quaestiones Homericae*, 24.3–5

Box 22: Another Heraclitus, 1st century AD, writes in his *Homeric Questions* about his namesake, our Heraclitus, the dark one (quoting sayings known as fragments 62 and 49a).

Here, in the second quotation in Box 22, Heraclitus seems to assert two contradictions: we do and we don't step into the same rivers; we are and we are not. What might he mean? The idea that we don't (or indeed can't) step into the same river twice is famously associated with Heraclitus, and seems to be linked to the idea that the river (like the world in general) is always on the move. You step again into what seems to be the same river, but it is not the same water into which you step. Is the river a body of moving water? If so, you step in again, in the same place, but into something different from what was there before. Or is the river something that remains though its water changes? Heraclitus prompts us to wonder

21. The River Caÿster at Ephesus. Did Heraclitus himself step into this very river?

whether perhaps the identity of the river is not just an issue of the matter: perhaps we do, in some sense, still step into the same river, even though it is not the same water. We do and we don't; it is and it isn't.

And we ourselves, what are we? Are we continuously the same matter, or do our bodies subtly change just as the water in a river drifts by, looking always much the same? What is it, indeed, to be *the same* from day to day? Perhaps, like the river, we both are and are not what we once were.

Both thoughts lead in the direction of supposing that in our world things are not defined so much by unchanging matter as by fluid sequences – that the 'things' that really matter (selves, households, families, political parties, value, time, money, power, and activities) are not quantities of persisting matter at all, but patterns of continuity in change. Why not suppose that things, not just rivers but, indeed, ourselves, and these other important things, are always simply patterns, patterns that are contextually identifiable, just as we found good and bad, up and down, and day and night, all might depend upon your point of view, in the quotations in Box 21.

Fire

In Chapter 2 we saw that the traditional story of the development of Presocratic philosophy places Heraclitus before Parmenides, and it suggests that Heraclitus used the element known as 'fire' to serve as the first principle of the physical universe, as though he, like other early thinkers in that story, was out to explain the material continuity of the world. But is this really so?

As we have just seen, a number of texts suggest that Heraclitus was pointing out that matter is not the basis of identity or continuity. On the one hand, we often identify the very same material object in quite different ways (drink or poison, uphill or downhill), and in other cases we identify *changing* matter as the same thing (the river, the sun, myself). Heraclitus sometimes mentions fire as one stage in a sequence of changes that occur in the world, a stage that recurs periodically over time either when the whole world is consumed by fire or when parts of it are kindled and cease to be what they formerly were. But fire is a consuming image, not an image of continuity. In the light of his interest in patterns of change rather than material identity, it seems wrong to take Heraclitus's recurrent fire as an underlying element, and better to treat it as a model for radical discontinuity of matter, where the motif of combustion allows Heraclitus to retain a pattern through the complete eradication of one stuff when another takes its place. Patterns occur in what (and how much of it) emerges after the destruction of something else. The process resembles burning (or indeed death).

Some key texts are in Box 23.

(a) Heraclitus makes it plain that he knows the world . . . is eternal by saying:

> This world, the same for all, neither any god nor any man made; but it always was and is and will be. Fire everliving, igniting in bits and going out in bits.

But the following text testifies that he also taught that it comes and goes:

> Turnings of fire: first sea; but from sea one half, earth, the other half, hurricane.

In effect he is saying that fire . . . turns into moisture – as it were the seed of the creation, which he calls sea – and that from this there comes earth again and sky and the surrounding materials.

Fragments 30 and 31, quoted in Clement of Alexandria, *Stromateis*, 5. 104.2–3

(b) Like the principle that organises the universe, it first substitutes the cosmos for itself and then produces itself again out of the cosmos:

> And all things are an exchange for fire, says Heraclitus, and fire for all things, like goods for gold and gold for goods.
>
> Fragment 90, quoted in Plutarch, *On the E at Delphi* 388DE

(c) Fire lives the death of earth, and air lives the death of fire, water lives the death of earth, earth that of water.

Fragment 76, quoted in Maximus of Tyre, *Lectures*, 41.4

Box 23: Fire and its role in the changing face of the cosmos.

In the quotation (b) in Box 23, Plutarch suggests that there are occasions when the whole cosmos goes out of existence, replaced by fire. But perhaps the most important feature of fragment 90, which he quotes there, is the analogy with trading goods for money. Purchasing goods involves exchanging one quantity of one kind of material (money or gold) for another kind of material (a gallon of petrol, perhaps). You hand over the money, you receive something else: the petrol is not the money disguised or altered to look like petrol, but a different commodity altogether. Just so we should suppose that the things in this world are not fire in disguise but are exchanged for fire and can be exchanged back again later. What remains (as in the trading example) is a certain value or measure – not the actual volume or weight, for we don't get the same *quantity* of petrol as we had of money – but its value in some other form, according to a regular exchange rate. This we often measure by the monetary value of the goods: 'I'll have five-pounds-worth of petrol', one might say. Likewise we can measure the quantities of each kind of matter, for Heraclitus, in terms of the amount of something else that you would get for them, and nothing is deducted in the process. 'Sea is poured forth and measures up to the same level as it formerly was, before becoming earth . . . ' (fragment 31 continued).

Logos: the word, the text, the reason

These reflections on the exchange rate for natural change direct us to the idea of a rationale or pattern to processes in the world; processes are fundamental, but they are measured processes. Everything flows, but it flows systematically. Opposites come and go, depending how you look at things, but there are patterns to how they emerge and what makes them significant. It is these patterns and the deeper harmony of structure underlying change that strikes Heraclitus most forcibly: this is what we should notice; this is what makes sense of the ever-changing world.

Heraclitus called the systematic structure which underlies every aspect of our experience '*logos*'. This multifaceted Greek word has many meanings, ranging from language, theory, and reason, to ratio, proportion, and definition. It is the word from which we derive our word logic, and the endings of science and knowledge words such as biology, geology, theology, and anthropology; in the New Testament it is used for the Word of God ('In the beginning was the *Logos* . . . ').

For Heraclitus, the *logos* is something that we need to learn to notice if we are to understand the true significance of the world. It manifests itself all around us but, Heraclitus suggests, only a few intelligent people ever realize what is going on. But what exactly is this *logos*? How are we to interpret what Heraclitus says about it? Indeed, how should we translate the word in any particular saying? The text in Box 24 is probably the opening section of Heraclitus's book, and the longest passage that we have. But what is he actually saying? Scholars still puzzle over this, generation after generation. Only the terms in italics are translations of the word *logos*.

> With this *theory*, which is for ever human, people are out of touch both before they have heard it and once first they have heard it; for although all things take place in accordance with this *theory*, they are like beginners experimenting with both words and practices such as these that I am going through as I divide each thing according to nature and say how it is. But it eludes other people what they are doing when they are awake, just as it eludes them what they do in their sleep.
>
> Heraclitus, fragment 1
>
> Box 24: Heraclitus's book supposedly began with these words, quoted by more than one ancient writer.

The main point here seems to be the failure of other people to identify what Heraclitus is trying to show them, both before he tells them and even afterwards as well. Yet what he tells them is something to which they ought, apparently, to be awake: they should not find it so unfamiliar, as though they were beginners trying something new. What is it? The *logos*, here translated 'theory', seems to be the rationale by which the world works ('all things take place in accordance with this *theory*') but people still can't get it, even when they have it pointed out. In some sense it is both Heraclitus's own theory or argument and also the measure or system which governs the processes in the world, which, as we have just seen, involves proportion and measure, systematic and quite obvious (to Heraclitus) patterns in the ever-flowing river of the world.

Heraclitus says that the universe is divisible, indivisible, created, uncreated, mortal, immortal . . . .

'Listening not to me but to the *logos* it is wise to agree that all is one,' Heraclitus says; and he complains that all men do not know this nor agree:

'They do not understand how in differing from itself it agrees with itself: a backward-turning stringing like that of the bow and the lyre.'

Hippolytus, *Refutation of all heresies*, 9.9.1–2, quoting fragments 50 and 51

Box 25: Hippolytus introduces Heraclitus's ideas, including the motif of the backward-turning *logos*. Look back to Box 6 in Chapter 2: can we be any clearer now on whether Heraclitus or Parmenides was the first to employ the term 'backward-turning'? Does it help that Homer referred to the bow as backward-stretched?

Heraclitus seems to have compared the *logos* that governs the behaviour of the world to the structure of a bow (for shooting arrows, for example) or a lyre (a stringed instrument functioning

22. The lyre was a stringed instrument played by plucking. The sound box was often formed from a tortoiseshell, as in the example at the centre of this scene. The strings were tightened by rotating a bar fixed across the two arms, creating a back-turning tension on the bent arms like that of a strung bow.

like a guitar). The key text is given in Box 25, and the crucial word that pinpoints the force of the image of the bow and the lyre is 'backward turning'. How exactly is the structure or stringing of a bow or a lyre 'backward turning'? Try to think what it is about these instruments that could be described in that way. What, then, would it mean when this simile is used to illustrate the *logos*?

Before Parmenides?

So was Heraclitus writing before or after Parmenides? As we discovered in Chapter 2, it is difficult to tell who is responding to whom from the way in which Heraclitus and Parmenides allude to each other's words. So are we now better placed to put them into a definite order on the basis of what we have seen in this chapter?

We have a sense that Heraclitus thrills to the perpetual flow of differences in the world: change is endemic, opposites flip into one another depending on your point of view, fire consumes what was there before and gives back something quite different. Nothing remains: the world exists in its pattern of dying and rising to new life, not in its material remnants. These patterns extend into religion, ethics, politics, and his analysis of language, on all of which he seems to have something to say (though it is often hard to grasp exactly what he means).

But if the whole world is a pattern of processes, surely we should not take Heraclitus to be a 'material monist', proposing a single underlying stuff. Did he think the world was really made of fire, as the first principles story at the start of Chapter 2 claimed? Does Heraclitus have anything in common with what Thales and Anaximenes had once been saying about the stuff of which the world was made? Or is he replying to Parmenides's stable and unified world with an alternative picture of his own, one in which nothing but the sequencing is the same? His system bears some resemblance to Empedocles's thesis of eternal recurrence, and what

Nietzsche found so familiar in Heraclitus was not a material cosmology but the tension of opposites that defined the world as a kind of warfare.

Perhaps Heraclitus lived before Parmenides, perhaps he lived after, perhaps he lived at the same time. Whichever way, his sayings cry out to be read in their own right, as a radically anti-materialist project unlike anything previously known. They bitterly resist the attempt to package them along with the pre-Parmenidean thinkers; they flourish in a situation in which we are able to juxtapose them with alternatives, such as Parmenides's world view, for which they may indeed have been a foil.

Chapter 6
Pythagoras and other mysteries

Philosophy has come to include, for us, a wide range of theoretical questions that typically look beyond what we can answer by experimental enquiries. While science asks how matter behaves, and tests its theories with observation, philosophy asks what matter is, or how observation can teach us anything. While mathematics asks what the sum of 2 and 7 is, philosophy asks what the number 2 is, and whether 2 plus 7 could ever make anything but 9.

These philosophical enquiries tend to be categorized in the modern world: we do ethics, or theory of knowledge; we do philosophy of mathematics, philosophy of language, or philosophy of religion. Many philosophers specialize in one or other branch of the subject. Yet even nowadays, the greatest philosophers tend to provide a whole new way of looking at the world, a system or vision which cuts right across the divisions within philosophy and offers an understanding of all the puzzles that have fascinated human beings. Philosophers of the stature of Kant, Hegel, Nietzsche, Wittgenstein, Descartes, Leibniz, and Hume did not just correct minor difficulties in a narrow part of the subject. They promised us a solution that would work for everything.

The same is true of the greatest among the ancient philosophers. One of the best candidates (and one of the earliest) from the Presocratic period is the famous 6th-century visionary Pythagoras.

Philosophers and mystics

Pythagoras has been somewhat neglected and despised in recent work on the Presocratics. One reason for this is that his vision of the world is characterized by an unusually personal style and a kind of mystical spirituality.

This is not to say that religious belief is incompatible with philosophical insight. Far from it. Standard commitment to the established rites of the local civic religion was normal in the ancient world, and not to participate would have been frowned upon. Indeed, there has been a long tradition, continuing to the present day, of reflective conformity to prevailing religious sentiments. Philosophers tend to recast the dominant religious doctrines to form a rational deductive system defensible from within the philosophical schools. But Pythagoras's spiritual adventures seem markedly different.

Although he was born in Samos, close to where Thales, Anaximander, and Anaximenes had recently been working, Pythagoras emigrated, as a young man, to Croton, in the southern toe of Italy (then part of the expanding Greek world). It was a region which seems already to have been steeped in a kind of religious fervour, with a strong interest in cults of the dead and in mystery rites associated with Hades and the Underworld. In Croton, Pythagoras soon established a sect of followers who took him as their guru, imitated his style, repeated his mantras, and kept his teachings a secret. What those teachings were exactly we shall never know. Many later writers tried desperately to sort through the mythology about this inspiring but elusive thinker, attempting to distinguish what was fact from what was imagination. They could find little firm evidence then, and we can find little now.

Thou shalt not kill nor eat

Whereas the standard religion of mainland and Ionian Greece was based around a cycle of civic religious festivals and official sacrifices, Pythagorean principles might appear to allow no space for animal sacrifice. From the testimonies in Box 26, we can see that immortality and reincarnation were fundamental motifs.

What Xenophanes says about Pythagoras goes as follows:

'And once, so they say, he was there
when a puppy was being beaten;
and he took pity and spoke these words:
Stop! don't strike! For it is the soul of a man, of my friend!
I identified it when I heard it squealing.'

Diogenes Laertius, VIII.36, quoting a poem (fragment 7)
by Xenophanes (c.580–480 BC)

The Egyptians are the first to have enunciated this theory that the human soul is immortal, and that as and when the body fails it repeatedly clothes itself within another creature that is being born, and when it has done the round of all the terrestrial, marine and flying animals, it once again puts on a human body that is being born; and the circuit takes it 3,000 years. There are some among the Greeks who adopted this theory as their own, some earlier, some later. Their names I know but I don't write down.

Herodotus (c.490–410 BC), *Histories*, II.123

Box 26: Early evidence for the doctrine of reincarnation. Was Herodotus avoiding naming Pythagoras? Why might he do that?

Pythagoras seems to have suggested that we (our souls) survive beyond death and are reborn in other bodies, sometimes as animals, sometimes as new human beings.

23. Ancient Greek cult practice included regular animal sacrifices, and the meat from the sacrifice would be shared among the worshippers. Pythagoreans, who practised vegetarianism, would exclude themselves from the ritual sharing of the communal meal.

Naturally, such a view makes our present life take on a different significance: this is not the only life we have, and how we live now may affect what we become hereafter. It also makes a difference to how we relate to other people and other species: people whom we don't recognize might be our dearest departed friends or the heroes of the past; animals we treat harshly might be our loved ones undisclosed.

Does it follow that we must be vegetarians and refrain from killing animals? Some texts suggest that Pythagoras was an advocate of vegetarianism on ethical grounds, because of the transmigration of souls into other animals; other texts suggest that sacrifice was not just part of the Pythagorean way of life but immensely important. The evidence conflicts, and it is hard to disentangle what Pythagoras himself believed.

In favour of the view that he was opposed to cruelty to animals we have the following:

- the poem, quoted in Box 26, in which Xenophanes imagines (for fun) Pythagoras objecting to the maltreatment of a small dog. If it is authentic, this is our earliest evidence concerning Pythagoras.
- the testimony of Empedocles, who was clearly inspired by Pythagoras and adopted a similar cycle of reincarnation for the soul. Empedocles was explicitly in favour of vegetarianism and opposed to animal sacrifice. The lines shown in Box 27 are usually thought to be about Pythagoras.

Pythagoras and other mysteries

But Pythagoras himself, having mastered the universal harmony of heavenly spheres and the stars that move upon them, heard the music of the universe, which we do not hear due to our small stature. It is to this that Empedocles testifies when he says about Pythagoras:

1　There was among them a man whose knowledge extended beyond limit
　　Who had acquired the longest wealth of wits,
　　And most effective at all kinds of clever works;
　　For whenever he strained with all his wits,
5　Easily he gazed upon each of the things that exist,
　　To ten human lifetimes and even to twenty.

For the words 'extended beyond limits' and 'gazed upon each' and 'wealth of wits' and the like are all particularly emphasising how Pythagoras's faculties of sight and hearing were uniquely and outstandingly accurate beyond other people's.

Porphyry, *Life of Pythagoras*, 30, quoting
Empedocles, fragment 129

Box 27: Porphyry in the 3rd century AD explains what Empedocles might have meant 800 years earlier when he wrote these lines, apparently in praise of Pythagoras.

Against the idea that vegetarianism is a necessary consequence of the Pythagorean reincarnation theory, we have the texts in Box 28, which suggest that sacrifice (apparently ordinary sacrifice of living things) was not just tolerated but placed as a high priority by Pythagoras himself and by the sect of followers who made it

(i) **Pythagoras of Samos visited Egypt and studied with the Egyptians. He was the first to import philosophy in general into Greece, and he was especially concerned, more conspicuously than anyone else, with sacrifice and ritual purification in sanctuaries, since he thought that even if, as a result of these practices, no advantage accrued to him from the gods, they would at least gain him a particularly fine reputation among men.**

Isocrates, *Busiris*, 28 (tr. Waterfield)

(ii) **The philosophy of the aphoristic group [of Pythagorean followers, often called *acousmatici*] is a series of aphorisms – unproved and unargued – to the effect that one must act in such and such a way, and they try to preserve all the other things that were said by Pythagoras, as divine dogmas. . . . This collection of aphorisms is classified into three types: some indicate 'what it is', some 'what most of all' and some 'what one must do or not do' . . . Instances of the 'what most of all' sort are as follows: What's the most moral thing? To sacrifice. What's the cleverest thing? Number, and second is he who gave the names to things. What's cleverest on our part? Medical skill. What's finest? Harmony. What's most powerful? Thought.**

Iamblichus, *Life of Pythagoras*, 82

Box 28: Reports that indicate Pythagoras's commitment to sacrifice.

their business to preserve his maxims and add nothing of their own. There is also the evidence in Box 29, about Pythagoras's reaction to a major breakthrough in mathematics.

Plainly we must not be too simple-minded. It will not do to jump to the conclusion that someone who holds a reincarnation theory, with transmigration of the soul into other animals, must necessarily be opposed to animal sacrifice. If Pythagoras believed in sacrifice, was he just irrational? It is worth stopping to think about the various ways in which his position could be defended to make it coherent. What unstated assumption are we adding when we suppose that reincarnation and animal sacrifice are incompatible?

Cycles of reincarnation similar to the Pythagorean one appear not only in Empedocles (Chapter 1) but also later in several of Plato's dialogues, put into the mouth of the character 'Socrates'. It is plausible that all these versions are inspired by Pythagoras, although since Pythagoras too may have borrowed the motifs from elsewhere, Plato's inspiration could be from other quarters. There seems little evidence to support Herodotus's speculations, in Box 26, that the original source was Egypt. Perhaps the ideas come from further afield, but it is equally likely that they derive from earlier Orphic practices which may have already existed in the region of southern Italy before Pythagoras got there, and indeed that such beliefs might be more common in other parts of Greece than our evidence has hitherto allowed us to recognize.

The magic of numbers

Pythagoras's name is best known today in connection with the theorem that, since antiquity, has borne his name. It provides a formula for calculating the length of any side on a right-angled triangle if the length of two of its sides are known – 'the square on the hypotenuse is equal to the sum of the squares on the other two

Apollodorus the mathematician says that Pythagoras sacrificed a hecatomb when he discovered that in a right angled
triangle, the hypotenuse squared is equal to the squares on
the two sides adjoining the right angle.

Diogenes Laertius, *Lives of the Philosophers*,
VIII 12

People who listen to those who like to investigate ancient
history will find them attributing this theorem to Pythagoras
and saying that he sacrificed oxen on the discovery.

Proclus, *Commentary on Euclid*, 426.1–9

Box 29: Two late sources associate Pythagoras with his famous
theorem. A hecatomb is a sacrifice of one hundred oxen: such a
sacrifice would have cost a working man all the wages of his
entire working life.

sides'. The first passage in Box 29 appears to take it for granted that
Pythagoras did discover this theorem, although it may not intend us
to believe the story about the sacrifice. The second passage is from
Proclus, writing in the 5th century AD. He does not explicitly
endorse the story even of the discovery, but he reports that one
would find it attributed to Pythagoras in books on the early history
of mathematics.

But what is it to discover a theorem? In one sense, it is to discover
(or deduce, or even posit) something that turns out to be true – in
this case that there is indeed a systematic relationship between the
lengths of the sides of a right-angled triangle. In another sense, it is
to demonstrate that your hunch is correct, by proving that it *must*
be so. It is interesting to reflect on how difficult it would be to
measure the lengths of lines on diagrams in the absence of precision
instruments for drawing or measuring; it is also hard to imagine
doing any theoretical geometry without first needing Pythagoras's
theorem as one of the basic tools for proving the lengths of all kinds

of other lines in other constructions besides triangles. So the discovery of the *likely truth* of Pythagoras's theorem is itself a major achievement (and useful in itself, if it turns out to have good results in predicting further truths).

The *proof* of the theorem would be another matter. It seems possible to believe that Pythagoras might have detected the truth of his theorem, without necessarily having discovered the proof of it. Of course, the notion of mathematical proof is an important prompt towards the development of logic, and towards the ideal of strict and valid proof in philosophical reasoning. But we do not *have* to attribute the notion of proof to Pythagoras, and we do not have to suppose that he himself discovered a valid proof for his theorem, in order to justify the claim that in some sense he might have *discovered* that there was such a relation between the lengths of the sides of triangles.

The discovery that the sides of the triangle, though not themselves invariably commensurate, are systematically related in their square powers must have been an exhilarating one. It probably deserves the sacrifice of a hundred oxen. It opens up the possibility that the entire world is based on hidden mathematical ratios that are not immediately obvious. This possibility is one that seems to have thrilled the Pythagoreans, and was reinforced by discoveries that they made about the ratios that underlie musical harmonies. Whether you measure the lengths of a plucked string, or the length and bore of a blown pipe, or the volume of a percussion object, it turns out that the sounds that we hear as harmonious with one another stand in certain simple mathematical ratios to one another: sounds an octave apart emerge from strings whose lengths stand in a ratio 2:1; sounds a perfect fifth apart emerge from strings whose lengths stand in a ratio of 3:2; and the ratio 4:3 produces what we hear as a perfect fourth. This is true no matter what length or pitch you start with, and it reflects the fact (unknown to the Pythagoreans, of course) that the wave frequencies of sound (to which hearing is sensitive) stand in those ratios for those intervals.

This truth is exciting, because it suggests a precise and scientifically verifiable link between what we find beautiful (perfect harmonies that sound easy to the ear, the kind of music we enjoy listening to) and real mathematical patterns in nature. You might have thought that taking pleasure in sounds was a matter of opinion. What seems beautiful to one person might not seem so to another. But it transpires that the beauty of harmony is an objective fact about nature, and it is a matter for calculation. It turns out to be a quantity as well as a quality. Perhaps, then, everything about the world, and every kind of good quality, is actually a matter of patterns of number? Science has followed this path with great success in the two and a half millennia since Pythagoras discovered it. Could moral, aesthetic, religious, and political values also be like

limit	limitless
odd	even
one	plurality
right	left
male	female
stationary	moving
straight	curved
light	darkness
good	bad
square	oblong

Box 30: The so-called Pythagorean table of opposites, as reported by Aristotle, *Metaphysics*, A 5. Finite/infinite and odd/even head the table, because the principles of mathematics are the foundations of all values.

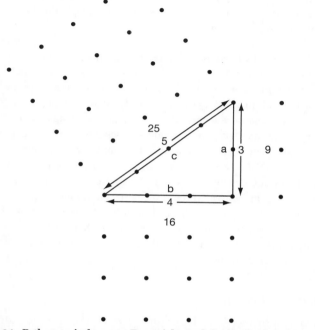

24. Pythagoras's theorem: *For a right-angled triangle, the square on the hypotenuse equals the sum of the squares on the other two sides.* Greek mathematics treated the task of squaring a number as exactly that, drawing a square diagram with a side the length of the number to be squared. By using pebbles or counters for the dots on this diagram, one could show that the square on the long side has the same number of evenly spaced dots as the two other squares put together. But sometimes the sum of the squares on the two short sides won't be a square number, and then the length of the hypotenuse will not be a whole number, and can't be represented with counters. So we can't use counters to demonstrate that the theorem is true in every case. To prove the theorem is true, the mathematician must resort to theory, since moving the pebbles round will only show that it works in the few cases where lengths a, b, and c are all whole numbers and commensurable. Even if Pythagoras did not find a proof for this theorem during his lifetime, he might have deduced that it is true.

that? Pythagoreans drew up a table of oppositions, founded on the contrast between even and odd in numbers. Is there any truth in the idea that the items in the left column of Box 30 have affinities with the 'odd' in mathematics and those in the right column have something 'even' about them?

Whether or not Pythagoras discovered his own theorem, it is certainly true that Pythagoras and his followers acquired a reputation for mathematical and geometrical investigations. They conducted their mathematics in a spatial way that strikes us as strange: numbers were conceived as lines, squares, triangles, and oblongs, laid out as patterns of counters or pebbles. The triangular number ten (composed of four rows of four, three, two, and one counter respectively) was special for several reasons: it is the sum of the first four numbers; it has the same length (four) on each of its three sides; it embodies all three of the perfect harmonies (octave 1:2, fifth 2:3, and fourth 3:4). This number had a special mystical name, *tetraktys*, and many of our sources report that the Pythagoreans were taught to swear their oaths by invoking the *tetraktys* as some divine force.

The perfect cosmos

It is tempting to link the Pythagoreans' interest in the *tetraktys* with what we know of their theories about astronomy. If we scan the sky on a starry night, it is obvious that the number and arrangement of the bodies visible from the earth cries out to be explained. How many are there? How far away are they? Are their relative positions fixed according to any regular pattern, or are they randomly distributed? Once you have the idea that number patterns can be found in nature, it is both natural and reasonable to search for the mathematical formula that lies behind the apparently scattered lights in the sky.

This is a task that is still going on, as scientists try to determine the distance of adjacent galaxies and link their pattern of distribution to

While most people say that the earth rests at the centre ... those of the Italian school, called Pythagoreans, say the opposite. For they say that there is fire at the centre, and the earth is one of the heavenly bodies which by circling round the centre creates the effect of night and day. And again they lay down another earth, opposite this one, to which they give the name 'anti-earth'. They do not look for theories and explanations in relation to the phenomena but they manipulate the phenomena in relation to certain theses and doctrines of their own, and try to make them fit together.

Aristotle, *De caelo*, 2.13, 293a18–28

At this time [i.e. the time of Leucippus and Democritus, see Chapter 4] and earlier the so-called Pythagoreans were the first to get a grip on mathematics and advance it, and being heavily involved in mathematics they took the foundations of mathematics to be the foundations of all that exists ... And they took the entire universe to be a harmonic scale and number. And those aspects of arithmetic and harmonics that they accumulated that were in accord with the processes and parts of the universe and with the entire cosmic arrangement, these they assembled and slotted in. And where there was some gap, they eagerly helped themselves to the idea that the whole system was consistent with their ideas. For instance, they say the bodies in motion in the cosmos are ten in number, because the number ten seems to be complete and to encompass the whole nature of numbers. Given that only nine such bodies are visible, they create the 'anti-earth' for this purpose.

Aristotle, *Metaphysics*, A 985b23–986a12

Box 31: Harmonic theory provides a model for extrapolating to the mathematics underlying cosmic phenomena.

accounts of how the universe might have come to its present form. But even in Pythagoras's day, it was clear that there were some bodies (the planets, sun, and moon) that occupy distinctive places relative to the earth. The solar system as we know it includes nine planets (earth among them) circling one sun: ten items. The ancients knew of only five planets, plus earth, sun, moon, and, beyond all that, what they took to be a dark sphere studded with fixed stars: nine items. As we can see from the texts in Box 31, the Pythagoreans deduced on mathematical grounds that the system ought to comprise not nine but ten bodies, and that the earth should, like the other planets, be a body in motion round a central focus.

The Pythagoreans were not the first to think of suggesting a pattern of numbers as key to the distances between the heavenly bodies (Anaximander had already made that breakthrough, a little ahead of Pythagoras). But in the Pythagorean speculations we can see that the notion of harmony, and the power of simple ratios in the *tetraktys*, has encouraged them to suggest that perfect patterns are what we would expect. Patterns will not be *almost* right, or *nearly exact*. Our observations and calculations may come out almost right or nearly exact, but the reality will invariably be exact. The fault always lies in observation, not in nature. This principle remains at the heart of experimental science, notwithstanding the provision in modern physics for certain kinds of irreducible uncertainty at the sub-atomic level (but only as a last – or perhaps temporary – resort, in the absence of any consistent theory that will successfully predict beyond a range of probability).

Mystics or mathematicians?

Most of our evidence for Pythagorean theory is late. The master himself wrote nothing down. His followers attributed everything to their great founder himself. It is hard to be sure what, if anything, is genuine Pythagorean teaching. Some later followers of the Pythagorean way, especially the important thinker Philolaus in the

5th century BC, can be credited with advanced theories of their own. But much of the content of so-called Pythagorean teaching appears to be a mix of mystical gobble-de-gook and adulatory veneration of the genius of the founder.

Besides the authenticity question, there is the question of what the essence of the Pythagoreans' way of life was. Was the rule against eating beans a mystical taboo, symbolic for some kind of detachment from worldly affairs? What kind of purity is assured by rules that say one must put on one's right sandal first and not walk on the main roads? Do these have hidden meanings, as many of the ancient reporters suggest? Or are they just special patterns of behaviour that mark out a Pythagorean devotee and test his devotion?

What did it really mean, to the ordinary Pythagorean, to be a follower of this way? That may be a question for social history. But it is hard to assess the significance of the movement's philosophical contribution without knowing what they thought, in their own minds, that they were trying to achieve.

Chapter 7
Spin doctors of the 5th century

In Chapter 2, our 'first principles story' ended with the words 'enter Socrates and the Sophists'. Socrates, of course, typically marks the beginning of a new period of philosophy in the textbooks. That is why we call the Presocratics 'pre-Socratic'. But most textbooks on Presocratic philosophy also allow some space to the Sophists, sometimes grudgingly, sometimes enthusiastically. To be sure, the Sophists have little place in the traditional first principles story. Their concerns are not easily fitted into the project described in that story, which was a project to explain the physical make-up and structure of the world. If the Sophists have any interest in that, it is to step beyond it, or even make fun of it, by questioning its very foundations.

But we have had reason to doubt that the first principles story is the only story we might tell about the motives and interests of intellectuals of the 6th and 5th centuries. The Sophists were certainly part of the intellectual scene in the 5th century (as also, incidentally, were an array of medical writers, historians, geographers, mathematicians, and others whose work we have not chosen to explore in this book).

'Sophist' means 'professional in cleverness', and it is their professionalism that marks these thinkers out as a group. History preserves the names of Protagoras, Gorgias, Hippias, Prodicus, and

Antiphon, among others. These were people who made their living by first creating a demand for intellectual skills and then charging a market rate for delivering them to the buyers. Now, for the first time in history, philosophy – if we can call it that – became a job, not just a leisure pursuit reserved for those with another source of income.

But of course, to make a living, you have to tap into the wealth of the moneyed classes in some way. It is no good creating a demand only among the poor, who cannot afford to buy the product, no matter how much they need it. This results in a paradox: the Sophists offered an expensive private education, yet the market for it thrived best in a democratic culture; they presented themselves as great facilitators of democratic procedures, yet their effect was to secure advantages for the well-to-do. 'Now,' said the Sophists, 'armed with this skill in words and ideas, you will be able to make yourself heard and believed in the courts and in the Assembly!' It was a message well calculated to chime with a democratic ideology, such as prevailed in 5th-century Athens. Where rhetorical ability, not noble birth, is the source of influence, anyone has the right to achieve that influence, whether they are rich or poor, whether they are of high or low birth. But of course, not everyone can achieve it in practice. Education in rhetorical skills can help to make democratic equality not just a theory but a reality. Or so you might suppose.

Yet it was not, in practice, the poor to whom the Sophists were addressing their sales talk; it was the rich. The Sophists' income had to come from the wealthy classes. So for all the democratic façade, their aim was really to appeal to those who would, under a less democratic system, have bought their way to power, or those who might have inherited influence by virtue of their aristocratic birth. When democracy is the prevailing ideology, the wealthy and the aristocrat cannot buy their way to influence directly. To retain their unfair advantage, they must buy it *indirectly*, by paying for an expensive education that gives them an edge over the ordinary folk.

So, if advantage is won by effective speaking in a popular assembly, then the way to win is to employ the winning words. And the way to do that is to learn it. And if learning it is expensive, so be it: one must pay. Thus the Sophists, spin doctors of all time, dressed their windows in democratic colours to hoodwink the poor while milking the rich. In return they taught clever talk designed to enable their pupils to manipulate popular opinion in their favour, and thereby maintain their plutocratic advantage in a system that was only nominally democratic.

So are the Sophists (and their modern counterparts) a good thing or a bad thing? Controversy has raged for more than 150 years, and fluctuates with the prevailing ideology of the contemporary world. Before the 20th century, while democracy was still unfashionable, the Sophists were generally condemned for their subversive effects, though Nietzsche admired them for promoting nature's winners to their rightful winning position. But by the 1950s the reverse was true. On the rebound from Hitler, liberal thinkers had come to distrust Plato for his potentially totalitarian political views. And if Plato was offensive, the Sophists, who were so often the butt of his attacks, came to seem less offensive. They began to be perceived as champions of liberalism, wrongly condemned by a Plato who was out to destroy democracy, equality, and freedom.

Perhaps surprisingly, this 1950s outlook has persisted almost unchallenged, and is regularly revived even today. It is nourished by a naive liberalism which assumes that totalitarianism and democracy are simple black and white alternatives.

But the time is surely ripe for a re-assessment. Social exclusion, economic disadvantage, and political spin all serve to render what is notionally a democracy quite undemocratic in reality. Public opinion can be a good guide to public policy only if the people are in a position to judge and can exercise their judgement freely. And freedom is no simple matter, since (as Gorgias himself argued, Box 35 below) rhetoric designed to seduce a listener into agreement appears to undermine autonomy. Paradoxically, the need to appeal

ALL THE
WORLD'S POOR
COULD BE FED,
CLOTHED, AND
HOUSED FOR
THE AMOUNT
THE WORLD
SPENDS ON
ARMS IN ONE
MONTH.

FROM
www.qu
DOM
THE

25. Democracy. People need to feel that they are free to express their opinions without pressure and without manipulation, and that their opinions are actually heard and make a difference. Rhetoric can help them to be heard, or it can help their oppressors to pull the wool over their eyes.

to the popular vote makes democratic leaders more inclined to engage in manipulation than autocratic leaders or hereditary peers and monarchs. By contrast, the autocrat, unlike the elected politician, can search simply for what is the best policy, without attention to whether it can be attractively packaged. Sophistry is one of the methods by which politicians dress up their policies in alien clothing, to pass them off as more desirable than they really are. Spin doctors thrive best where 'democracy' is the slogan.

Socrates and the Sophists

The dubious reputation of the Sophists is the tail side of a coin whose head side is the reputation of Plato and his portrait of Socrates. In the 4th century BC, when the great Sophists were all dead and gone, Plato wrote more than twenty dialogues, in many of which he creates a character called Socrates, based on the real Socrates (who had died in 399 BC). Many of these dialogues portray Socrates engaged in dispute with the best Sophists of his day. Plato brings out, in these imaginary conversations, various genuine worries about the political and ethical implications of the activities associated with the Sophists.

One recurrent worry expressed by Plato's Socrates was the idea that if one teaches for fees one must tailor what one teaches to what the paymaster dictates. Socrates, unlike the Sophists, charged no fees. And he, unlike the Sophists, was prepared always to speak his own mind (or would have spoken his own mind, if he'd known what it was). He did not care what people thought of him, and he was prepared to die rather than toe the popular line.

Besides the issue of academic freedom and integrity, Plato portrays Socrates exploring questions about knowledge (is opinion all that matters?) and ethics (is anyone's judgement as good as anyone else's?). Plato used fictional encounters between Socrates and the great Sophists as a setting in which he could dramatize Socrates debating these crucial questions. The discussions he invented

26. Law courts in Athens, such as the one that condemned Socrates to death, were run on democratic lines. A jury of 300 ordinary citizens decided whether the defendant was guilty, by a majority vote. There was no expert judge, and no professional lawyers. To win your case you needed to use the kind of rhetoric that would appeal to simple-minded folk, easily swayed by prejudice. Teachers of rhetoric cashed in on this need. Should Socrates have used Sophistic techniques to evade the death penalty?

highlight the shallowness and inadequacies in positions typically associated with the Sophists (for instance, that everything is just a matter of opinion, or that anyone is entitled to his own opinion and there is no such thing as falsehood). However, Plato's dialogues rarely present these matters as clear-cut, black-and-white cases. Generations of readers have looked for a simple answer that is 'Plato's view'. They have often read him, together with his character 'Socrates', as condemning the Sophists and all that they stood for.

If you hate Plato (or what you take to be Plato's view), you are likely to want to defend the Sophists as democratic heroes. If you like Plato, or the objections he attributes to Socrates, you will see the

Sophists as a threat to rational order. But the issue is really more complicated, and a less partisan reading of Plato can help to open it up. For the Sophists may indeed be a threat, not just to an extreme rationalist or totalitarian political order, but also to the kind of enlightened democracy that values equality of opportunity. And that ideal, which may be our ideal, is itself closer to what Plato favoured than you might think.

Some key themes in Sophistic thought

1. Nature and convention

Human societies typically organize their lives by means of norms and conventions which are respected by the members of the society and regarded as binding. Some of these count as laws and are enforced by penalties or sanctions; others are matters of decent behaviour or good manners and are enforced only by social sanctions, such as the good opinion of others. Once people notice that the way they do things here differs from the way others do them elsewhere, the issue arises as to whether these norms and conventions are really binding. Must we do the things that society tells us to do? They are, after all, just conventions.

The Greek word for a man-made law or convention was *nomos*. Many intellectuals of the second half of the 5th century in Athens became intrigued by the question as to whether such man-made laws could or should command respect. Where did they derive their value? And were there perhaps other (possibly conflicting) constraints or values that were *independently* and *naturally* right, not by mere convention but *by nature*? *Physis*, the Greek term for nature, captures this alternative source of value.

In the text in Box 32, Antiphon the Sophist suggests that conventions and laws directly conflict with what is naturally valuable. If so, and if we actually benefit only from the natural values, it would be better to disobey the conventions of society on any occasion when we can get away with it with impunity. It would,

27. We think of ancient Greek culture as the root of our own Western traditions, but some of their customs might take us by surprise. Men and boys trained in the nude, for instance. Here a strip of drawings portrays successive poses as a bearded athlete takes up his javelin and prepares to throw it, while another, standing by the altar, examines his discus. Men performed naked in the Olympic Games, and the nude statues were not a purely artistic convention.

Antiphon suggested, be all right to *seem good*, providing that really did bring genuine social advantages. But there was no point in *being good* when no one was looking. And in fact, he suggested, society does little to make life genuinely better for those who do act goody-goody. So on the whole, it was always better to seize any opportunities to act unfairly and steal the advantage.

> But this enquiry is entirely motivated by these facts, namely that the majority of things that are just according to convention are at odds with nature. For convention decrees for the eyes what they should see and what they should not see, and for the ears what they should hear and what they should not hear, and for the tongue what it should say and what it should not say; and for the hands what they should do and what they should not do, and for the feet what place they should go to and what place they should not go; and for the mind what it should desire and what not. But neither the things from which conventions divert the people, nor the things to which they recommend them, none of these is more attractive or suitable by nature. Life, on the other hand, is a matter of nature, and so is death, and life for humans arises from things that are beneficial, death from the ones that are not beneficial. But while things that are rendered beneficial by convention are constraints upon nature, those that are rendered beneficial by nature are liberty.
>
> Oxyrhynchus Papyrus, XI 1364,
>
> column 2. 23–4. 8

Box 32: Part of an investigation into the distinction between nature and convention by the Sophist Antiphon. Should we agree that total freedom to pursue natural advantages would be preferable to adopting human conventions that constrain our eyes, hands, and tongues?

This distinction between nature and convention crops up all over the literature and political thought of the late 5th century BC. Plato portrays an extreme version of it in the mouth of his

> The best and strongest among ourselves, these we mould by taking them young, singing to them, performing incantations, turning them into slaves, telling them that one must have equal shares and this is what is just and honourable. But if and when a man of sufficient natural stature turns up, he will shift aside all these conventions and break out and escape from the weight of them; he will trample over all our regulations, sorcery and fables and all the rules that go against nature. That slave of ours rises up and emerges as our ruler: there and then nature's own justice shines forth.
>
> Callicles portrayed in Plato, *Gorgias*
> (4th century BC), 483e–484a

> There is nothing for it: the feelings of devotion, self-sacrifice for one's neighbour, the entire morality of self-renunciation must be taken mercilessly to task and brought to court . . . There is much too much sugar and sorcery in those feelings of 'for others', of '*not* for me', for one not to have become doubly distrustful here and to ask: 'are they not perhaps – *seductions*?'
>
> Friedrich Nietzsche, *Beyond Good and Evil*
> (AD 1886), tr. Hollingdale, p. 33

Box 33: Callicles, a Sophist portrayed in Plato's *Gorgias*, is echoed 2,300 years later by Nietzsche. Both suggest that the genuine achievement of the greatest human beings is not *conforming* with what the herd thinks of as morality, but *breaking free* from that and daring to assert one's own right to rule. Is this a reversal of morality (there *are* moral rules but they are the opposite of what we supposed), or the abolition of morality (since nature's way is not a moral way at all)?

character Callicles, in the dialogue called *Gorgias*. There Callicles argues that man-made laws inhibit us and prevent us from exercising our natural capacities to the full. Indeed, worse still, the conventions are a vicious plot on the part of nature's born losers: the weaklings have ganged up to devise a way of keeping down those who were born to be great. By teaching children from an early age to be fair and not to take advantage of the weak, they instil an artificial sense of conscience. This, Plato's Callicles reasons, deters people from doing what they really want to do, which is to win as much as they can for themselves, at the expense of everyone else. That is how democracy, the rule by nonentities, gets going; it thereby ousts the rule by great tyrants that would be natural in the cruel world of nature, the world in which the winners win and thrive, and the losers lose and die. Only cowards, Callicles concludes, would let those inhibitions stand in their way.

2. Man is the measure

In another dialogue, *Protagoras*, Plato portrays Protagoras employing the nature/convention distinction in an early exercise in political theory. Protagoras is probably the most famous of the 5th-century Sophists. Plato's portrait is plausibly authentic. It shows Protagoras taking a more favourable attitude towards convention than Antiphon and Callicles, who had suggested that we were better off escaping from the constraints of convention.

Protagoras, by contrast, appears to have been in favour of conventions. He was famous for saying: 'Man is the measure of all things: of things which are, that they are so, and of things which are not, that they are not.' The word 'man' here translates a generic word for 'human person', not a male person specifically. Protagoras probably meant that we humans (or perhaps our shared human conventions) are the measure or yardstick for deciding what counts and what doesn't count as real. The world is as we make it out to be.

We might read 'man' in 'man is the measure' as a reference to human society as a whole. If so, Protagoras meant that the conventions of your society determine for you what does and what doesn't count as a matter of importance. Or we might read 'man' as a reference to the individual, operating in his own individualistic world, about which he is himself authoritative. If so, Protagoras meant that each of us is a perceiver looking out at the world, and what we see is up to us. It is not fixed by any independent reality. There is no shared world.

Either way, Protagoras appears to say that there is no independent truth about what things exist, or what they are like, apart from the way human beings construct them for themselves. In other words, the entire world is a construct of ours: we might say there is no 'nature' in the way that the nature/convention dichotomy holds.

We may be tempted to take Protagoras as more postmodern than he really was. Most of his own texts are, as ever, lost, but the opening words of his work on the gods (shown in Box 34) seem to imply that there might be a fact of the matter about the gods (whether they exist and what they are like) which is inaccessible to us, but still might be true. Would Protagoras have opened the discussion in that way if he had been intending to argue that the gods were merely a human construct? What ought he to have said, if he really meant that it's just up to you whether you view the world from a religious point of view or not?

Nevertheless, even if he was not a committed relativist about the gods, Protagoras's views on morality seem to have inclined towards relativism. If we are right that he held that societies form their own codes of moral conduct and legal systems, and that what was right for one society need not be right for another, it was a position that lent itself well to the profession of Sophistry. Suppose that nothing is absolutely right or wrong. Suppose that law and morality appeal to nothing beyond the opinions of the prominent individuals who make up the rules. Then surely it would be legitimate to argue

Protagoras, being a friend of Democritus, picked up Democritus's atheist doctrine. He's said to have employed the following opening gambit for his treatise about the gods: 'Concerning the gods, I am not able to know, neither whether they exist or not, nor what kind of form they take. For many factors stand in the way of knowledge: the obscurity, and human life being so short.'

Eusebius, *Praeparatio Evangelica*, 14. 3. 7

Box 34: Is Eusebius right that Protagoras speaks as an atheist here? In fact, both Protagoras and Democritus (see Chapter 4) seem to have allowed that gods might *be* there, but unknown to us, and perhaps unconcerned about us as well.

whatever one could get away with, in court and in the political assembly. What could be wrong with defending what had hitherto been considered immoral? If one succeeded, then it would no longer be considered immoral. But then, if it were no longer *considered* immoral, it would no longer *be* immoral. 'Immoral', after all, just meant 'disapproved'. Thus the morally unthinkable soon becomes thinkable. Nothing is sacred.

3. The power of persuasion

Rivalling Protagoras for notoriety in the pen portraits provided by Plato, the great master of rhetorical persuasion, Gorgias, is also the most entertaining of the 5th-century Sophists. Box 35 provides a sample of his showpiece speech in defence of Helen of Troy. The speech took an amusing theme ('Write a defence speech for the naughtiest woman ever'). But the work also has a more serious aim. It explores and illustrates the corrupting power of words.

Gorgias compared the power of words to the effect of drugs or physical force. Being overpowered by something beyond one's

If she was abducted by force, unlawfully assaulted and wrongfully violated, it is obvious that the man who abducted her is the wrongdoer, qua violator, while she, being abducted, is a victim of misfortune, qua violated. . . .

What then holds us back from supposing that Helen too came under the influence of words, against her will, just as if she had been taken by force? For . . . speech lacks the appearance of compulsion but it has the same power. Speech, by persuading the mind, constrains it both to believe what is being said and to consent to what is being done. Hence the man, by persuading her, is doing what is morally wrong in so far as he compels her; the woman, being subject to compulsion by the speech, we blame in error. . . .

The power of speech has the same relation to the configur-ation of the mind as the hierarchy of drugs has toward the nature of the body. For just as various of the drugs expel various humours from the body, and some terminate an ill-ness and others terminate life, so also some speeches sadden the listeners, some gladden them, some terrify them, some rouse them to valour, while others poison the mind with some kind of evil persuasion and seduce it. Thus we have outlined how Helen was not immoral, but unfortunate, if she was persuaded by speech.

> Gorgias, *Encomium of Helen*, excerpts from 7–15
>
> (the text is uncertain at points)

Box 35: Gorgias tries to persuade the listener that a person who persuades the listener deprives the listener of her judgement and power to resist.

control absolves a person from any kind of blame. You don't blame a woman for being raped by force. So why blame a person who is convinced by sweet talking?

Gorgias's speech is itself an attempt to overpower us, using words to take away our judgement: Gorgias attempts to work on his audience the very seduction of which he warns us in the text. Indeed, it was probably far from obvious, to 5th-century masculine listeners, that a woman raped by force was innocent, or that the man who took her by force was wholly to blame. Gorgias works his magic, in Box 35, first to convince his audience that the rapist must be wholly to blame. Though that point may have been new to his first audience, it has some justice to it. His next claim, however, that persuasive speech carries the same power as violent force, is distinctly dubious. Could we not be held to blame if we naively fell for the sales talk of a confidence trickster? Should we exonerate those who commit war crimes under the influence of political propaganda? Does advertising completely undermine our autonomy?

Of course, Gorgias has a point. He rightly alerts us to the insidious effects of exposure to rhetoric. But might we not still be responsible for allowing ourselves to be taken in? Shouldn't Helen have closed her mind to the smooth talk? To persuade us of his conclusion, that Helen was wholly innocent, Gorgias has to convince us that no one could ever resist being corrupted by words. Can we resist his specious argument?

It must be clear to every reader that the *Encomium of Helen* is a *jeu d'esprit*, designed to defend the indefensible, and to demonstrate or illustrate the power of rhetoric. More controversial is the only other work by Gorgias of which we have a substantial record, called *On nature or what is not*. The title was a pun on the classic texts of early philosophy, typically called *On nature or what is*. 'What is' means 'reality', or what exists. Parmenides's famous poem probably circulated under this title.

28. Helen of Troy being abducted by Paris. This event precipitated the Trojan War. But did she go of her own accord?

In *On nature or what is not* Gorgias presents a spoof work of philosophy designed to convince us that (a) there is nothing, and (b) – to make matters worse – even if there was anything, we could never know about it, and (c) – the last straw – even if we could know anything about it, we could never communicate it to anyone else. The joke is, of course, against *us*, since just in so far as Gorgias gets his message across he convinces us that what he has just done is impossible. Rhetoric is so powerful that it can not only convince you of the most bizarre thesis on earth: it can also achieve the impossible! It can convince you that the very thing it has just achieved is logically excluded.

An extract from the first part of this delightful piece of high-brow intellectual humour is given in Box 36. It shares some of the qualities of Parmenides's and Zeno's logic-chopping arguments against common-sense views about reality (see Chapters 2 and 3). But could it have been intended seriously? Many commentators have tried to take it as serious philosophy, and have attributed its nihilist and sceptical theses to Gorgias himself.

If you take that line, Gorgias emerges as a man who believed that nothing existed and that knowledge was impossible; a man who thought that the frivolous fallacies that his treatise contained were inescapable examples of good logic; a man who preferred to embrace its nonsense conclusions, rather than take them as a reductio of his hilariously bad reasoning.

Two reasons seem to me to argue powerfully against that conclusion. One is the sheer pedantry, as illustrated in Box 36. Not satisfied with refuting each of the two options in a pair of exhaustive alternatives, Gorgias always insists on offering a third alternative, for instance that both alternatives might be true together, and proceeds pedantically to offer a third proof, against that contradictory position (despite the fact that no serious thinker would have defended it). Whereas real scepticism always tries to

Besides, if it has being, it is either single or multiple; but since it is neither single nor multiple, as will be demonstrated, then something with being does not have being. For if it is single, it is either a discrete quantity or a continuum or a magnitude or a body. But if it is any of these, it is not single: if it is a quantity it will divisible, and if it is a continuum it will be severable. Likewise, if it is conceived as a magnitude, it will not be indivisible. And if it is in fact a body it will be threefold, because it will possess length, breadth and depth. But it is absurd to say that something with being is none of these things, and from this it follows that something with being has no being. Nor is it multiple, because if it is not single, it is not multiple either, because anything multiple is composed of singles. Therefore if there is nothing that is single there is nothing that is multiple either.

And so it is evident that neither does something with being have being, nor does something without being have being. And next it is easy to work out that it is not the case that both something with being and something without being have being.

Gorgias, *On what is not*, reported by Sextus Empiricus, *Adv Math*, VII 73–75 (tr. Waterfield)

Box 36: Gorgias exhausts the possibilities for reality, and concludes that none of them will do.

address the doubts someone might seriously be prepared to entertain, Gorgias has gone on to address positions that no one seriously recommends. A scepticism antagonistic even to nonsense looks like either a school exercise or a joke. One might compare the artificial exercise entertained in Descartes's *Meditations*.

The second reason against taking this text as a serious contribution to metaphysics is that it makes a very fine piece of work when it is read as an exercise in another area of philosophy. One area which we know Gorgias held dear is the investigation of the power and effect of words. We have already seen him exploring that topic, in the *Defence of Helen* (Box 35). Suppose, then, that *On what is not* is an attempt to take on the toughest task rhetoric has ever faced. Suppose its task is to defend a totally crazy and logically indefensible set of quasi-philosophical theses, theses that cannot be proved with genuinely sound arguments. Now try to spin a superficially convincing web of pedantic arguments so mind-boggling that they trap the unwary into confused defeat. Succeed, and you have once more (as in the *Helen*) demonstrated the totally overpowering way of words. But the exercise works only if you do *not* yourself believe the theses for which the defence is to be offered; if the magic is worked by persuasion not by logic; and if the arguments are not as good as they purport to be. The joke works just in so far as it is a joke that the author does not himself believe.

Of course, even if we believe that Gorgias wrote it as a joke, and that he did not believe a single one of the conclusions for which it appears to argue, yet we may still hold that, on the way, he spotted some good points (as well as some bad ones). It might even include some genuine philosophical insights. Gorgias's best contributions to analytic philosophy come in the observations about language in the third part of the work (and again, since the power of language is Gorgias's acknowledged interest, it is plausible that this would be the area in which he had most to contribute).

An extract from this part appears in Box 37. We don't need to accept his conclusion, but the problem that he raises, about how words relate to things, is indeed an important one.

> Language is that by means of which we communicate, but language is not the objects and things out there. So we don't communicate the things out there to our neighbours. We communicate language, which is something other than the objects. And so just as what is seen could not come to be something heard and vice versa, so also since the things themselves lie outside us, they could not come to be our language; but since they are not language, they cannot be communicated to another.
>
> Gorgias, *On what is not*, reported by Sextus Empiricus, *Adv Math*, VII 84–5

Box 37: Gorgias observes that words and things are different. So how is it that we can use words to pass on knowledge of things? Philosophy has not finished working out the answer to this one.

And the spin-off . . .

As the Presocratic philosophers bow out and Plato arrives to direct the next drama in the series, the Sophists make an astounding final act. All singing, all dancing, they ask society to question its *raison d'être*, its political beliefs, its moral values, its religious beliefs, its educational system, its legal codes, and its codes of etiquette. They draw attention to the power of the media and ask us to consider whether, without the media, there would be any truth at all. The antagonism that they generate, as portrayed by the Socrates imagined in Plato's dialogues, starts the ball rolling for some of the most exacting philosophical endeavours the world has ever seen.

Whether it was all spin, or a genuine intellectual movement, the Sophists must be given due credit. The spin-off which their outrageously unconventional attitudes generated, namely academic philosophy as we know it now, has never lost its momentum, over a period of 2,500 years.

Epilogue:
A story about origins

From Aristotle onwards, generations of philosophers have turned to the Presocratics in search of the origins of their own philosophical project. If we follow Aristotle we are likely to seek the origins of our subject, philosophy, in the Presocratics' searches for what they called *archai*, or origins. Aristotle emphasized the fact that the Presocratics looked for the origins of the physical world. He suggested that they were focusing above all upon what he called the 'material cause'; that they were attempting to explain why things are as they are on the basis of what things are made of. After the Presocratics, Aristotle thought, other philosophers identified other kinds of explanation, until he, Aristotle, had perfected the analysis of causation in his doctrine of the four causes.

Aristotle's account of the origins of philosophy remains immensely influential. That is not surprising since much of our evidence for the Presocratic period derives from Aristotle himself, or from writers such as Simplicius who were explaining Aristotle's ideas for later generations. It is understandable that the story still has a faintly Aristotelian air. Indeed we inevitably privilege the evidence we do have over material that is lost but which might have fleshed out other areas of the Presocratics' work, had it survived.

As we saw in Chapter 2, historians of philosophy in the 19th and 20th centuries developed a story of the origins of philosophy, in which the search for first principles, *archai*, was a key theme. Their story borrowed Aristotle's scheme which divided early Greek philosophers into two categories, monists and pluralists. They then added to that static picture a developmental model largely absent from Aristotle's synoptic picture. Presocratic philosophy was told as a tale with a before and after: thinkers were monists or pluralists because of their position in a sequence and their need to answer the challenges of their predecessors. As we saw, this story gave a key role to Parmenides, whose objections to plurality and change supposedly provoked the pluralist response in Anaxagoras and the atomists. The give and take of ideas emerged as a kind of debate between thinkers engaged in answering the same question, and in that sense too Presocratic cosmology could be presented as embryonic philosophy – the origin of what we do now.

In this book I have tried to resist the pull of Aristotle and the 19th-century formula. I have made an attempt to sketch out alternative stories in which issues other than the material explanation of the origin of things figure. I have sought to give adequate weight to the religious side of Empedocles's ideas; to the mathematical investigations of Zeno and Pythagoras; to the contrast between appearance and reality and its significance in the development of the theory of knowledge; to the metaphysical aspects of the themes in Parmenides, Melissus, and Heraclitus, such as their interest in change; and to the meaning of the word 'real'. Just as the story told by Aristotle reflected his own sense of what was important in his philosophy, so my focus in this book has reflected what I take to be important in the development of philosophy and what I think we owe to the Presocratics.

You may think that my story comes out rather less well focused than the first principles story. It is not so neat. And the thinkers seem to sail past each other like ships in the night, each one developing his own self-contained world view, or exploring issues that fire his own enthusiasm.

But if our subject, philosophy, grew out of the searches of the Presocratics, we need not suppose that their searches were confined to just one area of our current subject. There is not just one story to tell. Indeed we should suspect that for every area of the discipline that we now define as philosophy, our Presocratic predecessors took some faltering steps. The tradition has been selective in how much attention it gives to each part of their work, but it is up to us to look back and pick out what seems significant. We have to make the stories that we need out of the motley collection of material that has been passed down to us. We need those stories in order to explain the origins of our own endeavours, and to continue the task of understanding.

Further reading

Collections of translated texts

J. Barnes (ed. and tr.), *Early Greek Philosophy* (Penguin Classics, 1987).

Robin Waterfield (ed. and tr.), *The First Philosophers* (Oxford World's Classics, 2000).

Patricia K. Curd and Richard D. McKirahan, Jr (eds.), *A Presocratics Reader* (Hackett, 1996).

Commentaries with translations

Richard D. McKirahan, Jr, *Philosophy before Socrates: An Introduction with Texts and a Commentary* (Hackett, 1994).

G. S. Kirk, J. E. Raven, and M. Schofield, *The Presocratic Philosophers* (Cambridge University Press, 1983).

General works

Stephen Clark, 'Ancient Philosophy', in *The Oxford History of Western Philosophy*, ed. Anthony Kenny (Oxford University Press, 1994), pp. 1–54.

Edward Hussey, *The Presocratics* (Duckworth, 1972).

David Furley, *The Greek Cosmologists*, vol. 1 (Cambridge University Press, 1987).

J. Barnes, *The Presocratic Philosophers* (Routledge, 1979).

Texts and commentaries on individual thinkers

J. H. Lesher, *Xenophanes of Colophon: Fragments* (*Phoenix* supplementary vol. 30, Toronto, 1992). Text, translation, and commentary.

Charles H. Kahn, *The Art and Thought of Heraclitus* (Cambridge, 1979). Greek text of the fragments, translation, and commentary.

T. M. Robinson, *Heraclitus: Fragments* (*Phoenix* supplementary vol. 2, Toronto, 1987). Greek text, translation, and commentary.

A. Coxon, *The Fragments of Parmenides* (Assen/Maastricht, 1986). Text, testimonia, translation, and commentary.

Brad Inwood, *The Poem of Empedocles*, revised edition (Toronto, 2001). Greek text, introduction, translation of the fragments and testimonies; includes the new papyrus.

C. C. W. Taylor, *The Atomists Leucippus and Democritus: Fragments* (*Phoenix* supplementary vol. 36, Toronto, 1999). Greek text, translation, and commentary.

Gorgias, *Encomium of Helen*, ed. D. M. Macdowell (Bristol Classical, 1982). Greek text and translation.

Empedocles and the new papyrus

Alain Martin and Oliver Primavesi, *L'Empédocle de Strasbourg: introduction, édition et commentaire* (De Gruyter, 1999). The official publication of the Empedocles Papyrus; written in French with English summary (pp. 339–48) and including a reconstructed Greek text with translations into English and French.

P. Kingsley, *Ancient Philosophy, Mystery and Magic: Empedocles and Pythagorean Tradition* (Oxford University Press, 1995).

The Milesian philosophers and the beginning of philosophy

E. Hussey, 'Ionian inquiries: on understanding the Presocratic beginnings of science', in *The Greek World*, ed. A. Powell (Routledge, 1995), pp. 530–49.

Charles H. Kahn, *Anaximander and the Origins of Greek Cosmology* (Columbia University Press, 1960).

Kathryn Morgan, *Myth and Philosophy from the Presocratics to Plato* (Cambridge University Press, 2000).

Xenophanes and the gods

Sarah Broadie, 'Rational Theology', chapter 10 in *The Cambridge Companion to Early Greek Philosophy*, ed. A. A. Long (Cambridge University Press, 1999), pp. 205–24.

R. C. T. Parker, 'Greek Religion', in *The Oxford History of the Classical World*, ed. J. Boardman *et al.* (Oxford University Press, 1986), pp. 254–74.

Xenophanes and the problem of knowledge

E. Hussey, 'The beginnings of epistemology: from Homer to Philolaus', in *Epistemology* (*Companions to Ancient Thought*, vol. 1), ed. S. Everson (Cambridge University Press, 1990), pp. 11–38.

J. H. Lesher, 'Early interest in knowledge', chapter 11 in *The Cambridge Companion to Early Greek Philosophy*, ed. A. A. Long (Cambridge University Press, 1999), pp. 225–49.

Heraclitus

Catherine Osborne, 'Heraclitus', chapter 3 in *Routledge History of Philosophy*, vol. 1, *From the Beginning to Plato*, ed. C. C. W. Taylor (Routledge, 1997), pp. 88–127.

Daniel W. Graham, 'Heraclitus and Parmenides', chapter 3 in *Presocratic Philosophy*, ed. Victor Caston and Daniel W. Graham (Ashgate, 2002), pp. 27–44.

Alexander Nehamas, 'Parmenidean Being/Heraclitean Fire', chapter 4 in *Presocratic Philosophy*, ed. Victor Caston and Daniel W. Graham (Ashgate, 2002), pp. 45–64.

Parmenides and after

J. Barnes, 'Parmenides and the objects of inquiry', chapter 9 in his *The Presocratic Philosophers* (Routledge, 1979).

K. Reinhardt, 'The relation between the two parts of Parmenides' poem', in A. P. D. Mourelatos (ed.) *The Presocratics* (Anchor Books, 1974), pp. 293–311.

Patricia Curd, *The Legacy of Parmenides* (Princeton University Press, 1998).

Zeno's paradoxes

G. Vlastos, 'Zeno of Elea', in *The Encyclopedia of Philosophy*, vol. 8, ed. P. Edwards (Macmillan, 1967); reprinted in G. Vlastos, *Studies in Greek Philosophy*, ed. D. W. Graham, vol. 1 (Princeton University Press, 1995), pp. 241–63.

Richard Sorabji, *Time, Creation and the Continuum* (Duckworth, 1983), chapter 21.

Melissus

David Sedley, 'Melissus', in *The Routledge Encyclopedia of Philosophy*, ed. E. Craig (Routledge, 1998).

Anaxagoras, Empedocles, and the atomists

Daniel W. Graham, 'Empedocles and Anaxagoras: Responses to Parmenides', chapter 8 in *The Cambridge Companion to Early Greek Philosophy*, ed. A. A. Long (Cambridge University Press, 1999), pp. 159–80.

C. C. W. Taylor, 'Anaxagoras and the atomists', chapter 6 in *The Routledge History of Philosophy: vol. 1, From the Beginning to Plato*, ed. C. C. W. Taylor (Routledge, 1997).

David J. Furley, 'The atomists' reply to the Eleatics', in his *Two Studies in the Greek Atomists* (Princeton University Press, 1967), pp. 79–103; reprinted in A. P. D. Mourelatos (ed.), *The Presocratics* (Anchor Books, 1974), pp. 504–26.

C. C. W. Taylor, 'The atomists', chapter 9 in *The Cambridge Companion to Early Greek Philosophy*, ed. A. A. Long (Cambridge University Press, 1999), pp. 181–204.

Pythagoreanism, mathematics, and harmonics

Carl A. Huffman, 'The Pythagorean tradition', chapter 4 in *The Cambridge Companion to Early Greek Philosophy*, ed. A. A. Long (Cambridge University Press, 1999), pp. 66–87.

Ian Mueller, 'Greek arithmetic, geometry and harmonics: Thales to Plato', chapter 8 in *The Routledge History of Philosophy*, vol. 1, *From the Beginning to Plato*, ed. C. C. W. Taylor (Routledge, 1997), pp. 289–314.

The Sophists, democracy, and rhetoric

Robert W. Wallace, 'The Sophists in Athens', chapter 9 in *Democracy, Empire and the Arts in Fifth Century Athens*, ed. Deborah Boedeker and Kurt A. Raaflaub (Harvard University Press, 1998), pp. 203–22.

Paul Woodruff, 'Rhetoric and Relativism: Protagoras and Gorgias', chapter 14 in *The Cambridge Companion to Early Greek Philosophy*, ed. A. A. Long (Cambridge University Press, 1999), pp. 290–310.

Jacqueline de Romilly, *The Great Sophists in Periclean Athens*, tr. J. Lloyd (Oxford University Press, 1992).

G. B. Kerferd, *The Sophistic Movement* (Cambridge University Press, 1981).

G. B. Kerferd (ed.), *The Sophists and their Legacy* (Wiesbaden, 1981).

J. Ober, *Mass and Elite in Democratic Athens: Rhetoric, Ideology and the Power of the People* (Princeton University Press, 1990).

B. Vickers, *In Defence of Rhetoric* (Clarendon Press, 1989).

Index

Expand your collection of
VERY SHORT INTRODUCTIONS

Visit the
VERY SHORT INTRODUCTIONS
Web site

www.oup.co.uk/vsi

➤ **Information** about all published titles

➤ News of **forthcoming books**

➤ **Extracts** from the books, including titles not yet published

➤ **Reviews** and views

➤ **Links** to other **web sites** and main OUP web page

➤ Information about **VSIs in translation**

➤ **Contact** the editors

➤ **Order** other **VSIs** on-line

ANCIENT PHILOSOPHY
A Very Short Introduction
Julia Annas

The tradition of ancient philosophy is a long, rich and varied one, in which a constant note is that of discussion and argument. This book aims to introduce readers to some ancient debates and to get them to engage with the ancient developments of philosophical themes. Getting away from the presentation of ancient philosophy as a succession of Great Thinkers, the book aims to give readers a sense of the freshness and liveliness of ancient philosophy, and of its wide variety of themes and styles.

'Incisive, elegant, and full of the excitement of doing philosophy, Julia Annas's Short Introduction boldly steps outside of conventional chronological ways of organizing material about the Greeks and Romans to get right to the heart of the human problems that exercised them, problems ranging from the relation between reason and emotion to the objectivity of truth. I can't think of a better way to begin.'

Martha Nussbaum, University of Chicago

www.oup.co.uk/vsi/ancientphilosophy

PHILOSOPHY
A Very Short Introduction
Edward Craig

This lively and engaging book is the ideal introduction for anyone who has ever been puzzled by what philosophy is or what it is for.

Edward Craig argues that philosophy is not an activity from another planet: learning about it is just a matter of broadening and deepening what most of us do already. He shows that philosophy is no mere intellectual pastime: thinkers such as Plato, Buddhist writers, Descartes, Hobbes, Hume, Hegel, Darwin, Mill and de Beauvoir were responding to real needs and events – much of their work shapes our lives today, and many of their concerns are still ours.

'A vigorous and engaging introduction that speaks to the philosopher in everyone.'

John Cottingham, University of Reading

'addresses many of the central philosophical questions in an engaging and thought-provoking style ... Edward Craig is already famous as the editor of the best long work on philosophy (the Routledge Encyclopedia); now he deserves to become even better known as the author of one of the best short ones.'

Nigel Warburton, The Open University

www.oup.co.uk/isbn/0-19-285421-6

CLASSICS
A Very Short Introduction
Mary Beard and John Henderson

This Very Short Introduction to Classics links a
haunting temple on a lonely mountainside to the glory
of ancient Greece and the grandeur of Rome, and to
Classics within modern culture – from Jefferson and
Byron to Asterix and Ben-Hur.

'The authors show us that Classics is a "modern" and
sexy subject. They succeed brilliantly in this regard …
nobody could fail to be informed and entertained – and
the accent of the book is provocative and stimulating.'

John Godwin, *Times Literary Supplement*

'Statues and slavery, temples and tragedies, museum,
marbles, and mythology – this provocative guide to the
Classics demysties its varied subject-matter while
seducing the reader with the obvious enthusiasm and
pleasure which mark its writing.'

Edith Hall

www.oup.co.uk/vsi/classics